IMPROVING
Your
COMMUNICATION
☛ Skills

IMPROVING

....Your

COMMUNICATION

☛ Skills

SECOND EDITION

MALCOLM PEEL

KOGAN PAGE

Acknowledgement

I would like to put on record my most sincere thanks to Bob Norton, Head of Information Services for the Institute of Management, for his preparation of the Bibliography, and his helpful comments and advice on Chapter 11.

First published 1990
Second edition 1995

business communication
communication skills.

Kogan Page Limited
120 Pentonville Road
London N1 9JN

British Library Cataloguing in Publication Data

A CIP record for this book is available from the British Library.

ISBN 0 7494 1542 8 Pbk
ISBN 0 7494 1719 6 Hbk

Typeset by DP Photosetting, Aylesbury, Bucks
Printed and bound in Great Britain by
Clays Ltd, St Ives plc

Contents

Introduction

'Our communication,' roared the Chief Executive to his subordinate directors, 'is dreadful. I want it improved immediately.'

The Director of Office Services went away and ordered a brand new internal telephone network for £1m. 'That's not what I meant at all,' said the Chief Executive, and sacked his Director of Office Services.

The Director of Personnel went away and drew up a brand new organisation structure, complete with both solid and dotted lines. 'That's not what I meant at all,' shouted the Chief Executive, and sacked his Director of Personnel.

The Director of Computing and Information Technology went away and bought a network of micros and a comprehensive suite of interactive, real-time software. 'That's not what I meant at all,' screamed the Chief Executive, and sacked his Director of Computing and Information Technology.

The Industrial Relations Director went away and set up a magnificent Consultative Procedure to ensure continuous contact between Management and Employee Representatives by a daily cascade of briefing meetings. 'That's not what I meant at all,' roared the Chief Executive, and sacked his Director of Industrial Relations.

No sooner had he done this than the Chief Executive suffered a violent heart attack and found himself standing before the Great Head of Communications in the sky. 'If none of your fellow directors understood you,' asked the GHOC, 'do you think the failure in communication that you observed could have had anything to do with you?' It took only a little physical communication from a subordinate with a red-hot toasting fork to persuade the Chief Executive just how true this was.

The importance of communication

Like breathing, eating and the other processes of life, communication is essential to survival.

From the moment of birth, and possibly even before, we are enmeshed in a web of communication. Through communication we learn the skills of survival and self-development; the more effectively we communicate, the better our chances in every aspect of life. Through communication (or lack of it) we make friends and enemies, woo a partner, earn our living and enjoy our leisure.

Effective communication is at the heart of leadership; leaders cannot exist without followers, and leaders and followers are bound together by chains of communication. The best leaders in every field are highly effective management communicators and command the ability to get through to others, both inside and outside the organisation.

The better we communicate in our private life, the more smoothly that life will run. The most intimate relationships are made or broken by communication.

We communicate as long as we are alive; we cannot opt out. Even if we were to sit motionless and unresponsive, we would communicate an attitude to those around us, to which they in turn would react. Lying asleep snoring communicates to those observing us: utter exhaustion or too much wine with lunch, according to context. The question is not whether we choose to communicate, but how effectively we do it.

Communication skills

Communication skills, therefore, are among our most important life skills. They are a product of the abilities we are born with and what we have done to develop those abilities.

Some people hate writing letters, or are petrified by the need to speak in public. Some are afraid of the telephone, or unable to get a point across in a heated argument. Others are capable of setting an after-dinner audience rolling in the aisles, or of writing a best-selling novel. But whatever the level of our communicating skills, we can make them better, given only the wish to do so and help such as this book offers.

The plan of this book

This book does not promise to turn you into a world-famous dramatist or orator, but it will provide the basis for improving your communication skills in all the most common areas. The approach is practical and based on well-tried methods. While most examples are drawn from business situations, almost everything is also relevant to leisure activities and private life.

Because it aims to cover as many types of communication as possible, some sections may be too basic, too detailed, or irrelevant to your needs. If so, please pass quickly and selectively on.

Chapter 1 sets out the essential elements common to all kinds of communication. Part 1 (Chapters 2 to 6) covers face-to-face communication in a variety of situations. Part 2 (Chapters 7 to 9) is concerned with written communication. Part 3 (Chapters 10 to 12) deals with communicating equipment and machinery. Each chapter contains a list of dos and don'ts.

Sexism

I have used the masculine forms throughout only to save the reader endless repetition of his/hers, etc, or the tiresome use of long-winded and evasive expressions. No sexist connotation is intended at any point.

Chapter 1

The Elements of Communication

From the definition of 'communication' as: 'Imparting or exchange of information' (*The Pocket Oxford Dictionary*) we might think that it is a simple activity. But it is not. Communication is one of the most complex activities we ever undertake.

Six elements are essential to any complete act of communication. There must be:

- sender
- message
- system
- language
- context
- receiver.

If, as a manager, I say 'Come to my office, please.' I am the sender; the message is that I want the person spoken to to come to my office; the system is my voice; the language is spoken English, and the context the office in which it is said. The receiver is the person I am speaking to.

In writing this book, I am the sender; the message is what I believe will help you to communicate more effectively; the system is a complex one involving my hands, my word processor, the publisher, the printer and distributor; the language is written English; the context is the present day world of business; and the receiver is you, the reader.

We will now look briefly at each.

The sender

The sender of a communication is, or should be, in the driving seat. The initiative is his, and with it the responsibility for success or failure. For

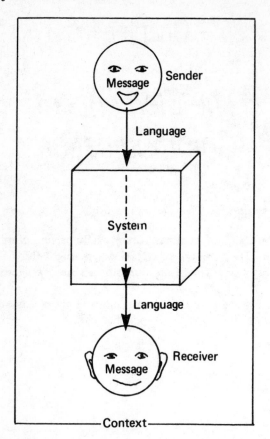

The elements of communication

this reason, any attempt to improve communication must concentrate on the sender, even though each of the other elements is also important.

The sender chooses

The sender chooses message, system and language, and decides how to use each to best advantage.

We may have little direct control over the receiver, but we must exercise any control we can. To communicate effectively we must think *not* of what we want to say, but what we want our listener to hear. We must put ourselves in his position, and plan our communication so that it will reach him in perfect condition.

The context may be harder – even impossible – to control, but the skilful sender will be aware of the context of his attempted communication, and do anything he can to manipulate it to his advantage.

Timing can be critical. If the receiver is occupied with something else, we must make it clear that our message is important. If he is asleep, then we must shout loudly enough to wake him. If the receiver doesn't read English, we must write in a language he understands.

The sender is affected

The sender is affected by making a communication. Indeed, it may well have more effect on him than on the receiver. 'A trouble shared is a trouble halved.' 'Confession is good for the soul.' Talking about problems is one of the best ways we can help ourselves to find our own solutions. The psychiatrist's couch and the confessional booth are examples of situations in which communication is more important to the sender than to the receiver.

All messages affect the sender in some way; they satisfy a need, or they would not have been made. In thinking about how, when and whether to communicate, we must consider our own state of mind, and our reasons for wishing to do so. Holding forth to a colleague or friend because we are annoyed about something that does not concern him, for example, may do more harm than good.

The sender may also be the receiver

The sender may be the same person as the receiver. Most of us write ourselves notes, keep diaries and address lists, and these days carry Filofaxes.

Thought is a sort of internal communication, and has the same elements: we consult our memory and feelings; we are aware of what our senses tell us; we debate ideas; we affirm conclusions.

The sender's status

The perceived status of the sender affects communication.

If a known hoaxer, such as the boy who cried 'Wolf', called out 'Help!' the message would communicate only that 'He's at it again.' If the cry was by someone we respected and admired, who had never, in our hearing, previously cried out for anything, we would give it our immediate attention. In fact, both senders might be in the same degree of trouble, but the action we took would be very different.

The importance of the sender's perceived status is also demonstrated by the credence given to spoof stories on TV and in the press. The belief in the media as trustworthy communicators overcomes our natural scepticism, even when we are aware that the date is 1 April.

The same can be true in any communicating situation. At a meeting, for example, the reaction to an attempted contribution – even whether it is heard – depends on the status and respect accorded to the speaker.

The message

Messages may appear to be simple things, but they rarely are. Like icebergs, the bulk of a message often lies below the surface.

A message need not be a statement, but can be an invitation to the receiver to make a statement; that is, a question. Questions are an important element in communication. In face-to-face communication, especially interviews, their effective use can be crucial. The role of the question is discussed in the appropriate chapters.

The content

A message must make sense, both to sender and receiver.

If the sender regards his messages as boring – he is attempting to send them only because he must – he is unlikely to communicate them effectively. If the receiver regards them as boring, the chances of communication are reduced even further.

Messages may be what the hearer expects, or unexpected. They can be welcome or unwelcome. How effectively they communicate depends to a large extent on what they contain; an after-dinner audience at the Rugby Club is unlikely to take in much of a lecture on Chinese syntax.

We may wish, as a manager, to ensure that a subordinate takes a certain course of action. But depending on our character, his character, the situation and our relationship, there are many ways we could structure the message. We could say:

> *'I want you to do this.'*
>
> *'My director wants it done this way.'*
>
> *'Do you feel this would be the best thing to do?'*
>
> *'Unless you do this, I shall consider disciplinary action.'*
>
> *'Everyone will be delighted if you do this.'*

and so on. While the core is the same, these are very different messages.

Emotion

The 'meaning' of a message is rarely pure matter of fact. Emotion rears its head almost every time. Whether it is part of the message as sent, or generated in the receiver, few messages are without it. This emotional component of messages is one of the most troublesome problems of communication.

In instructing the subordinate on what to do, we may feel a variety of emotions; impatience, anxiety, the desire to help or confidence. The subordinate's feelings might include resentment, gratitude, doubt or boredom.

The emotional effects of a message are not confined to private life, but are strongly evident in business communication. Industrial relations, bargaining and negotiation, taking and giving orders, personal assessment, remuneration, giving and responding to leadership, personnel selection, decision-making – all involve emotion in the sender, the receiver or both.

The emotions people feel control how a communication works. If we feel strongly, we may misunderstand it or even reject it. If someone criticises something we have done, we may:

- mishear what he is saying
- reject what he says out of hand
- misunderstand his reasons
- form an instant dislike of the speaker.

For such a communication to succeed, the sender must, therefore, use great care.

However, emotion also affects communication in less obvious cases. The worst traps are where the sender does not realise what the feelings of the receiver may be. To discuss education, for example, with a teacher who has just been made redundant may not result in the communication we intend.

If we want to communicate effectively, we must always consider emotion, in ourselves and in the others involved. It is not always easy to be sure how another person will feel about a message, but the better we can guess the more able we will be to communicate.

What is not included

In some messages what is not said, but might have been, is more important than what is said. This can be the case, for example, in testimonials and personal references, which list favourable aspects but do not mention unfavourable ones. To remain quiet when we are expected to speak will convey a clear message: 'I know more than I am prepared to say', 'I want nothing to do with you', 'You are not worth bothering with', 'I'm sulking.'

Disinformation

Communication is not always positive. Lies, whether of the white or black variety, are a common and important class of message. Most governments use propaganda, and some resort to brainwashing and reprogramming.

The system

We may think of communication simply as the transmission of information. But any complete system of communication includes means of finding, transmitting, storing and retrieving information.

The human system

The basic system for communication is the human body; not only the organs of speech and hearing, but eyes and facial muscles, hands and arms, brain and in many respects the entire body.

Touch. From birth onwards much of the most important communication is by touch: caressing, embracing, holding hands, punitive and other violence, even dancing. It is no coincidence that normal social and the most intimate personal communication are both described as 'intercourse'.

While much communication within the family is by touch, this also has a place in the most businesslike environment. In the western world, the firm handshake, the pat on the back, the reassuring pressure on the shoulder have a role in social and business life.

Body language. This is only a recent term for something we use throughout our waking hours. Everyone can interpret a blush, a threatening gesture, tension in the hands or round the mouth, and so on. Smiles, nods and how we stand or sit often communicate far more, and far more accurately, than any words we may utter. It is often possible, through observation, to understand more about a conversation we cannot hear, at the far side of a room, than if we heard the words.

Other actions. 'Actions speak louder than words.' Apart from touch and body language, we also communicate through direct action. We can, for example, offer a helping hand to someone carrying an awkward load; pick up an object he has, knowingly or unknowingly, dropped; open a door, or perhaps shut it in his face; we can pour him a drink; allow him to precede us; block his path. All these, and many other actions, communicate a powerful and immediate message.

The voice. The voice communicates more than simply the words spoken. If we shout, the message will not be the same as if we whisper. Looks and gestures convey at least as much as the words. 'Come to my office, please' said warmly with a smile is not the same message as 'Come to my office, please' muttered between clenched teeth, and emphasised by a commanding gesture. If 'Come to my office, please' was said softly, by someone with a gentle smile on his face, it might communicate an invitation to friendship, even intimacy.

'Come to my office, please' can convey a threat of trouble, a promise of reward, total uncertainty, or a range of specific meanings. Which is most likely may be judged by the tone of voice, facial expression and possibly gesture.

Information technology
The term 'information technology' has been hijacked by the electronics industry, thus creating an unnecessary and unhelpful mystique. Mechanical aids and hardware of various kinds have been used to help communication since the dawn of history. In this century, electronic communication in all its ramifications has become one of the biggest sectors of the economies of the developed world. This subject is discussed in more detail in Chapter 11.

Informal communication
We must not allow ourselves to think of communication as occurring only through formal, planned systems: nicely phrased letters, carefully constructed reports and laid-down channels.

There is also in every group, organisation or community a web of informal communication, which sets its tone and does a great deal to affect how it works. This web – the grapevine, gossip, rumour, reputation, whispers, 'little birds' and so on – is often more powerful than any official communication system could ever be. To communicate effectively in any organisation or community we must be aware of this, know how it works, and use it.

The language

A language is a system of symbols or sounds used to convey meaning. We tend to think first of language as communication by words, but there are many other types.

The computer has accustomed us to languages or codes consisting of numbers, possibly of 0s and 1s only. Music, sign language, pictograms, logos, house styles and colours, coats of arms, devices, insignia, numbers, equations, chemical symbols, codes of all kinds including such well-known varieties as morse and semaphore; all these perform, at least partly, the function of language.

Thought is only partly verbal. We may think in words, but we certainly think in pictures, and possibly in other ways as well. Dreaming and the activities of the subconscious and unconscious mind are probably, for most of us, non-verbal activities.

This is of practical importance in trying to improve our communication skills. We must not concentrate too much on words at the expense of other 'languages' that may be at least as important. We should not be too academic; we live in a rough and complicated world, where effective communication is achieved by the whole person. Indeed, some people believe that the use of language as a prime tool of communication is now declining.

We will glance quickly at verbal languages and picture language. The important language of numbers – mathematics and statistics in all their forms – is too specialised for more than a mention here, as are computer programming languages, music and others.

Verbal languages
Verbal languages are the most important code used for communication, and words are the bricks of such languages.

Language is a basic tool of life, both for us as individuals and for the society we live in. It helps to hold together nations, races and cultures, and to make them different from others. It has political, class and sexist dimensions. The language we speak and the way we speak it indicates much about our place of origin, education, social background, profession, and possibly about our religion, intelligence and interests.

The better we can use language, the better we are able to communicate. The effective use of language involves knowledge of its words (including how they are spelt) and of the way they combine together, or what is called the grammatical structure or syntax of the language.

Language skills are partly general, and partly specific to the four separate areas of reading, writing, speaking and listening. Someone may, for example, have no skill whatever in the Chinese language, while in French he has good reading, moderate writing and speaking, and poor listening skill.

Communication in more than one verbal language is an increasingly important skill. English speakers have the advantage of knowing the most used language in the world today, just as those who knew Latin were strongly placed in the medieval world. But with this undoubted advantage come the dangers of arrogance and complacency. Those who will succeed best in the international business climate of tomorrow will have the skill of communicating with as many as possible of their contacts in their native language.

Picture language
'One picture is worth a thousand words' is only partly true. There are no rewards for trying to convey complex meanings with words, when a drawing would communicate immediately and accurately. We must enlist the aid of maps, plans, graphs, charts, engineering drawings and other statistical drawings whenever they can help. Symbols may convey meaning more readily than words, and mean the same to virtually every nationality.

Apart from insight, pictures also stimulate interest; most people when handed an unknown book immediately thumb through to find any pictures. We must use this factor in our communications.

The receiver

The role of the receiver, whether reading, listening, or using another sense, is the most neglected aspect of communication.

Rebuilding the message out of the signals received (like a TV set recreating images from the wave-forms) requires time, patience and intelligence. Whether we are listening to a friend, a lecture or a favourite piece of music, reading a report or a book on communication, we must work for success.

Reading skills
We fall into the trap of assuming that, after lessons at primary school, everyone can 'read'; that a well-sent message will automatically be

International signs

received. But we all have a limit to our English language reading skills; if you doubt this, try reading, for example, a book on modern philosophy.

Other barriers to reception

Poor reading or listening skills are not the only barrier to reception of a message. To shout 'Help!' very loudly does not, sadly, guarantee that we will be saved. If the only person within earshot is stone deaf, fast asleep, engaged in some absorbing activity, or in mortal peril, our chances of survival are slim.

The efficiency of people's senses also varies. They may be chronically deaf or colour-blind. They may have a heavy cold. They may be distracted by worry or illness.

The receiver's objectives and expectations

Receivers also have objectives; they are not merely 'hearers'. A mother will pick out the sound of her baby crying in an upstairs room, despite the hubbub of the party going on around her. Out of the many we can hear at any one time, we all select which message we listen to.

The same is true of sight. Out of the many images our eyes receive, we select those, sometimes tiny and hard to focus on, which we believe to be of importance or interest. This is one reason why so many of us are bad photographers. We expect the camera to behave in the same way as our eyes and brain, by enhancing the section of a landscape that matters to us, and are disillusioned when it does not.

All receivers have a tendency to hear or read what they expect or want to hear or read – not the message actually sent. People often read a news item or report, for example, as confirming their own point of view when in fact it opposes it. The preconceptions which filter messages and affect their interpretation are sometimes known as 'frames of reference'. Several people receiving the same message will almost certainly interpret it differently according to their individual preconceptions or frames of reference.

The context

The physical and psychological contexts both affect how communications are received.

Our request for a subordinate to come to our office would stand little chance of communicating if a filing cabinet fell over, the fire alarm rang or an angry customer burst in at the same time.

Physical context

We will hear little of a presentation if the central heating system is receiving its annual decoke at the same time, or if a drama of life and death is being played out in view of the windows. For communication to succeed, there should be the minimum of distraction.

There may be little either sender or receiver can do about the context. Jamming the wavelengths to block radio communication may present technical and moral problems, and try as we may, we cannot calm the tempest or put the clock back. But if the elements are not within our control, at least we can try shouting during a lull in the storm. Timing, choice of mechanism, format of message and so on can sometimes be manipulated in order to overcome the problems.

Psychological context

The message conveyed also depends on everything that has gone before, and the relationship between sender and receiver.

'Come to my office, please' may be part of an ongoing message about managerial support, development of the individual and participative decision-making. On the other hand, it might be the latest in a series of warnings about inadequate performance, a further indication of egoism or an unsatisfied desire to dominate.

Knowledge of the context is essential to a correct reading of the message.

Part 1

Oral Communication

Chapter 2

Face to Face

Effective face-to-face communication is essential to every relationship: marriage, friendship, personal and business partnerships, parent–child, boss–subordinate, colleague and team-member. If communication fails, even on a single important occasion, the entire relationship can be in jeopardy.

Face-to-face communication gives more feedback and more chances to correct misunderstanding than any other method. Whenever we have the need for effective communication, whether in our personal life or at work, with people we know well or with complete strangers, when facing problems or sharing happiness, a face-to-face meeting is our first choice.

We will look at some guidelines for success, before turning to some of the commoner problems.

Guidelines for success

Success in face-to-face communication depends on a number of factors, including:

- setting objectives
- starting a discussion
- body language
- eye contact
- voice control
- listening
- the conventions of conversation.

Setting objectives

Even in everyday conversation, the more clearly we perceive our objectives, the better our chance of attaining them.

We may be aiming to persuade, to gain information about facts or attitudes, to get to know an individual, to strengthen (or break) a relationship, to initiate action, impress, amuse, or just pass the time of day. If the conversation is likely to be important, it is a good idea to jot down objectives.

Apart from our objectives, we should think about the general approach which is likely to work best in the particular situation. In a military briefing, for example, structured and formal exchanges would be expected. A difficult discussion between partners or close colleagues, on the other hand, would call for a sensitive, responsive and interactive approach.

Starting a discussion

Starting a discussion on a difficult subject can be a major problem. Many important issues, whether in business or personal life, have remained undiscussed for this reason alone. A common reaction is to postpone discussion 'until the moment is ripe', or hope for an opportunity to introduce the subject casually. Such approaches are usually self-defeating; we should plan to grasp the nettle.

Our opening must attract the attention of the other party, set the tone, and indicate (or state explicitly) our main objectives. We can adopt one of several approaches:

The formal opening. This is right when both parties know in advance that the conversation has been planned to take place and what its objectives are. For example:

> *'Thank you for coming, Peter. As you know, I felt we needed to talk about your frequent lateness . . .'*

Laying the groundwork is advisable before discussing a complex or potentially embarrassing subject. We should clear away misunderstandings, make our own position clear, and give a factual explanation to help understanding of the main subject:

> *'The management committee had a long meeting yesterday to discuss the development plan for next year. As you can imagine, the financial and budgetary implications were critical, and it became apparent there would have to be some departmental reorganisation. Just about every possible combination was discussed, but whichever way we looked at things, your area seemed a problem . . .'*

A brief introduction helps conversation on almost any subject, but pomposity or holding forth about our own views should be avoided. People also vary widely in the speed with which they focus their thinking, and it is frustrating to have to listen to an introduction when you have already grasped a situation fully.

A question can ease a conversation opening that would be difficult if attempted with a bald statement. For example:

'How are things at home these days?'

A direct statement is the easiest way into a subject, provided it is not too sudden or unexpected. However, we need to weigh up the other party carefully; some people react well to this approach, but others may be put off. It is most likely to be appropriate with someone we know well, and where there is mutual trust and respect. For example:

'Fred, I have a problem. Why can't you get here in time in the morning?'

The transition moves an existing conversation to a new area. It is a common and useful way of opening up an important or difficult subject. Sudden transitions sometimes work, but it is usually better to find, or create, an opportunity to move naturally from one subject to the next. Try to pick up a remark by the other party that can form a natural bridge to the subject you wish to raise:

'Yes, as you say, the M25 is getting worse week by week. Is this one of the reasons you seem to find getting here on time a problem?'

This approach can sometimes appear underhand, and if done clumsily in a delicate situation it will be counter-productive.

Body language

The way we use our bodies is of great importance in face-to-face communication. It can reinforce, weaken or perhaps completely contradict our words. If the mouth says one thing but the body another, it is the body that should be believed. We must, therefore, use our own body language to best advantage, and learn how to interpret the body language of others.

The messages the body can convey are powerful, but compared with speech, the range is crude and limited. The most common include:

- interest/boredom
- belief/incredulity
- liking/dislike
- tension/relaxation
- aggression/submission
- honesty/deceit.

Interest is shown by a responsive and appropriately changing facial

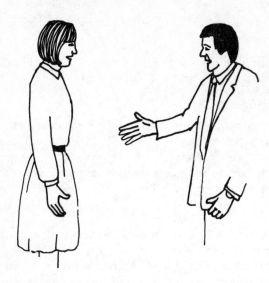

Handshaking. The initiator creates a psychological advantage

expression, nodding and noises of interest and agreement, looking at the speaker (or anything to which he is seeking to draw attention), leaning or turning towards the speaker, and holding the body still. *Boredom* is indicated by fixed or inappropriately changing facial expression, glancing away or at a watch or clock, shuffling papers, frequent change of posture, movement towards a door or exit, and in extreme cases yawning.

Belief is indicated by nodding, a relaxed mouth and a suitably responsive face. *Incredulity* produces shaking of the head, a tight mouth and widely opened eyes, or the deliberate touching of the nose.

Liking is shown by wide-open eyes, close continuing eye contact, a pleasant and responsive smile, a posture turned and open towards the speaker, possibly by movement towards or touching. *Dislike* is expressed by narrowed eyes, tense mouth, shut or turned-away posture and facial expression.

Tension is seen in small movements of the body, especially the hands, or occasionally by complete and unnatural stillness, forced posture and tight expression. In extreme cases it produces sweating. *Relaxation* is readily seen in posture and expression.

Aggression is seen in facial expression, glaring eyes, clenched fists, touching the face. *Submission* is indicated by downcast eyes, nodding or hunched shoulders.

Honesty can occasionally be deduced from a frank, open expression, while *deceit* from lack of or possibly over-insistent eye contact together with small, apparently purposeless movements. However, interpretation of body language is at its least reliable in this area, and should never be trusted in isolation.

Body language should always be read in the whole context of what is happening. But correctly interpreted and sensibly used observation of body language can do much to improve the effectiveness of face-to-face communication.

Eye contact

Biologically, the eye may be regarded as an exposed part of the brain, and together with the surrounding face, it is the most communicative part of the body.

Eye contact during face-to-face conversation normally occurs for between 50 and 75 per cent of the time, and forms a channel of communication at least as powerful as the voice. Not to look the other party in the eye – whether through shiftiness and dishonesty or shyness and uncertainty – weakens communication. The eyes convey an emotional commentary on what is being said and heard.

By maintaining good eye contact we keep this channel of meaning flowing, receiving and sending vital components of the conversation. If, on the other hand, we are not looking at the other party's eyes, we must either have ours closed or be looking elsewhere.

While closed eyes may occasionally be accepted as a sign of intense concentration, they are more likely to be seen as a sign of tiredness or extreme boredom.

The effect of looking elsewhere depends on the nature of the elsewhere, and whether the looking is done by the speaker or the hearer. A glance at a watch or clock will universally be taken as a desire to end the conversation. A glance at some other person or happening will distract the other party, and may be taken amiss. Both these actions are more damaging if done by the speaker than by the hearer.

The range of options for using our eyes during conversation is thus limited. If we are talking about some physical entity – a paper, an object, a view, another person or event – then to look at this while speaking or listening is acceptable, but even then we need some eye contact with the other party.

Resting our glance on a part of the person other than the face is distracting, offensive or suggestive, unless clearly appropriate to the conversation.

It is, of course, possible to use eye contact too intensely, and puzzle or even frighten the other party by making him feel he is being scrutinised or hypnotised. It has been suggested that more powerful and outgoing personalities use less direct eye contact than others. Whether this is so or not, eye contact is a delicate and important component of communication, and should be used thoughtfully and meaningfully, both to send and receive messages.

Voice control

The voice can be varied in loudness, speed and musical pitch. To communicate well, we must control all these.

Loudness must be appropriate. If we are trying to communicate across a large empty hall or a parade ground, we will need far more volume than if we were in a drawing-room or a small office.

If we are too loud, we will convey a threat or the feeling that we regard the other person as stupid. If we are too quiet, it will be hard for the other person to hear. We will cause strain and tension and risk misunderstanding. Most people are reluctant to admit they have not heard what has just been said, especially if the difficulty is repeated.

Problems with loudness usually occur when we misjudge the acoustics, or underestimate the noise around us. Any private conversation at a party, reception or meeting is in danger, especially if the room suddenly goes quiet. Curtains, hangings, vegetation, rows of empty seats or other furniture absorb sound, and such locations need special care.

The speed of speech is important. As with loudness, not only physical but emotional factors are involved.

From the physical point of view, if we speak too fast, the other party will not be able to follow all we say, and may not bother (or wish) to ask us to slow down. If we speak too slowly, the other party may become bored and edgy. He may allow his thoughts to wander or decide we are in need of help, interrupting and suggesting words to us.

Emotionally, misjudged speed of speaking may make the other party feel we are not bothered about how we communicate with him. He will suspect we feel that either the message or he is unimportant, and switch off or become angry or upset.

Within limits, speed and loudness are interchangeable; we need not speak so loudly if we speak slowly.

Listening

If communication is to succeed, the receiving side must work as effectively as the sending.

Admit failures

We should be ready to admit listening failures, whether in hearing or understanding. There is always a reluctance to do this, especially if understanding is the problem. We feel it will be seen as an admission of stupidity, and fear a reaction of impatience or even anger. However, we must face this if the attempted communication is at all important. For example:

> *'Sorry, John, I haven't followed you there. If Peter was so anxious to be helpful, why did you turn down his offer?'*

> *'Can I just make sure I understand you? I realise the computer disks are different sizes, but surely it is possible to get the contents transcribed?'*

By a frank admission, we will often discover that the facts or reasoning of the speaker are faulty, rather than our hearing or understanding. Whether we do or not, such an admission will be better than carrying on and hoping for enlightenment later.

Encouragement. Trying to talk to someone who does not appear to be listening has probably broken more marriages than adultery. If we wish all our relationships to flourish, we must find ways of seeming to listen, even on those doubtless rare occasions when our attention may be momentarily distracted.

Nods, smiles, grunts, repetition of a key word, good eye contact, positive interjections (such as 'indeed', 'I see', 'go on', 'yes!', 'yes?', 'I quite agree . . .'), an alert and upright posture, and an appropriate facial expression are all encouraging. They help the speaker to marshal his thoughts and words, and the listener to maintain his concentration. Properly used, they can turn an atmosphere of uninterest, boredom and non-communication into one of vibrant two-way exchange.

Keeping an open mind. It is essential to listen to what is actually said, rather than what we expect to be said. As explained earlier, all listeners have their individual 'frames of reference', depending on their knowledge, personality, preconceptions and experience. We cannot avoid this, but for accurate listening we should be aware of and allow for it.

The worst traps are when we have formed a strong preconception about the speaker or the subject under discussion. If, for example, we are convinced that the speaker has done something wrong, we will be in danger of failing to hear his evidence to the contrary. If we do hear it, we are likely to hear it less sensitively and accurately than evidence which appears to support the conviction we have formed.

The harmful effects on communication which can result from emotional involvement, either with the speaker or the subject, are discussed later in this chapter (pages 37–9).

Deafness. Listening is not the same as hearing, but if we cannot hear there can be no question of listening. Failure to hear clearly breeds suspicion; we tend to feel that information is being deliberately withheld, and this makes us resentful and distrusting.

Even at an early age, some people suffer from a degree of deafness of which they may be unaware. If we experience conversational problems, we should consider the possibility of a hearing defect, either in ourselves or the other party.

The conventions of conversation

Most people accept that to be productive and pleasant, conversation must be conducted according to conventions or generally accepted rules, but we rarely pause to consider what they are. This is an area in which manners and common sense work together; good manners are a sound basis for successful face-to-face communication.

The conventions include such items as:

- set up subjects by mutual consent
- talk in terms your hearer will relate to
- interrupt as rarely as possible
- don't use monologue
- don't contradict
- don't put words into another person's mouth
- use humour with care
- don't change a subject without preparation
- know how and when to stop.

Setting up subjects by mutual consent

Desultory exchanges such as a long-married couple may make during an evening in front of the TV are hardly a conversation, any more than occasional remarks made as work is processed in an open office. However, a conversation can grow from any of these if the seed drops on to fertile ground.

Subjects may be set up deliberately, designed to interest the parties present. This is often the basis of dinner-table conversation, when host or hostess sit those with common interests next to each other, or carefully throw remarks at those they judge likely to pick them up.

Many subjects grow from what might be called 'ground bait': remarks thrown into a discussion (or a silence) to test the reaction of the others present. News items, hot gossip, useless but remarkable information and controversial opinions may all serve this purpose. For example:

> *'I don't think much of this new form of yours.'*

may be greeted by silence, general merriment, angry exclamation, or used as the opening to a sensible conversation between two colleagues.

Problems arise when the situation is misunderstood by one party. One side might believe a conversation has been started as a constructive analysis of a problem among equals, while the other sees it as a reprimand.

Talk in terms your hearer will relate to

To attempt a conversation about the finer points of the latest computer with someone who has no interest in electronics is unlikely to result in satisfactory communication. We must test the ground before embarking on a subject the other party may be indifferent to or fail to understand. Of course, he may understand it better than we do. Whether he does or not, to sound patronising is as harmful as talking over someone's head.

The same difficulty can arise if we use jargon, abbreviations or simply buzz words which the other party does not understand. This will inevitably produce a feeling of separation, possibly of being deliberately put down.

Interrupt as rarely as possible

Interruption is always resented in the absence of some special reason such as the sounding of the fire alarm or a total misunderstanding of what has been said.

However, it is not always easy to judge whether a speaker has finished, and this may cause problems. It takes sensitivity and practice to get this right, especially if several people are anxious to contribute to a conversation. Correct observation of the speaker's body language will help, but there is no infallible rule except to wait patiently for silence. Apologise if you do interrupt: 'I'm awfully sorry . . .'

If we feel the speaker is deliberately or clumsily preventing anyone else from joining in, we may need to come in quickly when, as at some point he must, he pauses for breath.

Don't use monologue

To be forced to listen in passive silence to a monologue, however significant the views expressed, will kill any conversation. A listener's span of attention depends on the subject and the speaker, but rarely goes beyond a few minutes – two or three at most. In most conversations, speeches of no more than a minute are the longest that are readily acceptable.

If we are afraid of losing control by stopping, then something is wrong, but we will not correct it by trying to bludgeon our hearer into submission. For an effective dialogue, we must ensure that we pause often and invite reaction, feedback and involvement from the other party.

Don't contradict

Disagreement in conversation is inevitable and healthy. Indeed, if the parties do not bring different points of view, it will hardly be worth having. But this is not a licence for bald contradiction; disagreement must always be expressed with care.

In matters of fact, contradiction may be necessary, but we should (*a*) be quite certain of our own ground, (*b*) give our evidence or reasons, (*c*) let small or unimportant differences pass, and (*d*) put it politely. For example:

> *'Last month we exported over £100,000 of our new product.'*

> *'That's odd. I'm not sure where you could have got that figure. If I read it rightly, my sales return shows £65,000; see here . . .'*

In matters of opinion, contradiction is one of the most frequent and serious causes of failed communication. For example:

> *'The market survey our consultants carried out was a complete waste of time.'*

> *'It was not. It was one of the most interesting exercises I have ever seen.'*

Even a small change to the wording would give this exchange a better chance of being fruitful:

> *'I must admit that the market survey our consultants carried out seems to me to have been a waste of time.'*

> *'Sorry, but I can't go along with you on that. To be frank, I thought it was one of the most interesting exercises I have seen for a long while.'*

The differences are more than verbal. This time each speaker has implied that he is expressing an opinion, and thus cleared the way for compromise as the discussion proceeds.

Don't put words into another's mouth

There is a temptation during conversation to jump ahead when listening, assuming we know what is about to be said. For example:

> *'When I saw him doing that, I suddenly realised what he was really after, and . . .'*

> *'So you told him what you thought of him, and just what he could do with his idea.'*

There are several dangers here. The chance that the original speaker was about to use the words we have put into his mouth is small. If we are wrong, we have interrupted the speaker's thoughts, and suggested thoughts he may not have had. This may actually distort his view of the incident he is describing. Even if this is not the case, he may not be prepared to correct us; if he does, the rapport between us will be damaged and the flow interrupted; if he does not, we shall continue with a wrong impression.

Use humour with care

The way jokes, witticisms and humour in general are used is critical to effective conversation.

Any humour must obviously avoid comments that could offend – hence the general avoidance of race, religion and politics. There is always the danger that someone may be or choose to regard himself as the butt of a joke. While some people seem to adopt the role of conversational scapegoat happily, their acceptance may mask other feelings.

Self-deprecating remarks are usually safe, and as near to a sure-fire vein of humour as many of us have at our disposal, for example:

> *'I'm always slow on Mondays, but I must admit to being rather confused . . .*

However, if we misjudge it, such an approach will sound sarcastic or subservient.

In many conversations, it is bad manners to be serious; ideas are thrown around to extract as many opportunities for humour as possible. While the quality and quantity of humour will vary according to the talents of the individuals involved, it is usually best to avoid interjecting serious comment.

On the other hand, if a subject has been set up seriously, it can be ill-judged to use it as a source of humour.

Don't change a subject without preparation

Having originally set up a subject and a basis of discussion that is mutually agreed, we must be cautious about changes. Of course, any conversation can drift. For example:

> *'It's interesting you should say that. A similar thing happened to me only last week . . .'*

and away the speaker goes on a subject of his own, only tenuously related to the previous speaker's subject. Whether deliberately or not, the second speaker will have wrenched the initiative from the first, who may have had more to say.

This is acceptable within limits, but if the conversation is more than social chit-chat, these limits are fairly strict. Both parties to a conversation should stay with a subject until they feel it has run its course.

What is virtually always counter-productive is to make a pre-emptive strike to jump from one subject to another in mid-flow, although there are a few circumstances in which it can be right:

> *'Ooh look, that man has just stolen that woman's handbag . . .'*

> *'Sorry, that's the front doorbell . . .'*

Such a change is also worth trying if we sense a speaker is straying on to dangerous ground:

> *'I expect you feel the same as I do about your boss and his crazy ideas . . .'*

> *'Hang on a minute, it's just occurred to me that the VAT return is due today; have we completed it yet?'*

but such attempts are clumsy at best.

We may change the subject without intending to, in which case a quick apology will be appropriate:

> *'Sorry, I interrupted your train of thought. You were talking about . . .'*

Know how and when to stop

A conversation should not be left in mid-air. If it is worth having, it is worth finishing neatly and to the satisfaction of both parties. Equally, a conversation may be spoiled by going on too long, as many a salesman has found to his cost when the agreed sale has come unstuck.

There are many ways of ending a conversation. The most common is a jointly accepted conclusion:

> *'Yes, that's right. I think we can agree on that one.'*

This, of course, occasionally takes the form of an agreement to disagree:

> *'Well, I think we must agree to disagree, but at least we know each other's position.'*

Agreed action is another common conclusion:

> *'OK. I'll talk to Jenny this afternoon, you'll ring George up, and we'll compare notes tomorrow.'*

Lack of time or interruption can only result in an unsatisfactory end. If the discussion had any importance, it should be resumed at the point it had reached as soon as possible.

As with a social visit, so in a conversation it is polite to drop hints of our intention to draw to a close before we actually do so. Apart from giving tactful warning, this presents an opportunity to the other party to make any final points, or conversely to indicate that he feels there is more that needs discussing. Body language and movements such as rising, tidying papers, moving towards the door, may be appropriate.

Problems

Problems that may affect face-to-face communication include:

- emotional reactions
- distractions
- shyness
- fear
- unfamiliar situations.

Emotional reactions

This is the most common and most formidable barrier to effective face-to-face communication. Emotional reactions are not bad in themselves; they may be an important part, perhaps the very essence, of the communication. But they can get in the way, by twisting or even blocking out the message. They may arise from our feelings about the person with whom we are trying to communicate, from the subject of the communication, or from within ourselves.

Emotional involvement with the other person
We may feel love, distaste, fascination, distrust, loyalty, or any other of the vast range of human emotions. Emotional involvement with people is an inescapable part of our working as well as private life, and those who are tempted to feel otherwise deceive themselves.

Shop assistants or waiters serve those they approve of more promptly and with more care. At selection interviews, managers will listen more closely, believe more readily and judge more charitably candidates to whom they have taken a liking. Nurses and doctors will do more for those they see as 'good' patients. Even judges react to counsel they trust or cannot stand.

Many of the worst communication problems result from poor 'chemistry' between people who must work together. We all experience situations in which, for whatever reason, we are unable to get across to another person. These problems may be temporary or long-lasting; if long-lasting, they can have a deeply destructive effect on an organisation, and reach far beyond those directly involved.

In such cases action is essential. It may be possible to move one or both of those concerned, change working methods so they can avoid contact, or bring them together for a frank, direct discussion of the problem.

Emotional involvement with subjects
This is just as harmful, but can be harder to deal with. Any subject can generate a wide range of feelings: boredom, commitment, mastery, possessiveness and many others.

Such reactions may be unconscious; we may not even realise our involvement with a subject or the way it affects our communication. They can inhibit our understanding of an argument, make us selectively or totally deaf, or cause us to hear the opposite to what was actually said. We may express ourselves badly through anger, make wrong assumptions about our hearer, or indulge in biased thinking.

Examples of such problems are endless. Those with right-wing views will have problems when faced with evidence favourable to nationalised industry. The motoring enthusiast will hardly hear the praises of British Rail. The founder-director will be reluctant to respond logically to the arguments of a manager who believes the company's image is old-fashioned. The brilliant young graduate will have problems resolving the doubts of the canny and cautious old-stager.

The key to success in such situations is to be aware of our feelings and allow for them. Often it helps to bring them into the open early on, for example:

> *'You're touching a raw spot with me there, Mark. I was born in Yorkshire, and I happen to be very sensitive to criticism of the county and its people . . .'*

Emotional reactions within ourselves
Reactions that are not generated by other people or the subject may be caused by mood, unrelated events or longer-term problems. It is difficult to converse pleasantly, or even logically, when you have just been told that your spouse has left you for another.

Here again, the best strategy can often be to make the situation clear. For example:

'Sorry if I'm not at my best this morning – I was up most of the night taking cough medicine and things to Mary.'

However, there is always the danger of appearing to play for sympathy, especially if we are involved in a difficult conversation; we may judge it better to soldier on in silence.

It can be tricky to pick up such emotions in another person if he does not tell us. Our automatic reaction is to think that we, or something we have said, has caused the anger, annoyance, boredom or whatever; we should always consider whether we may be wrong.

Distractions

Distractions may be internal or external.

Internal distractions are of many kinds, ranging from the nearly permanent to the purely transitory. Communication is likely to be impossible with someone who has just lost a child or a job, is hungry or anxious to find a loo, or who has just dropped a heavy object on his toe. Some of these situations are self-evident, but it requires sensitivity to pick up the less obvious ones.

External distractions, such as a clap of thunder or a low-flying aircraft, are obvious to both parties, and therefore relatively easy to deal with.

Other distractions are serious and long-lasting, such as heavy traffic on the nearby road, or a television on in the same room. In such cases, important or difficult communication will require special care or even postponement.

Some may affect one party to a conversation only, such as an event happening behind the other's back, or a distraction of interest to one party only, such as the passing of a rare car to a motor enthusiast.

Background noise always makes communication harder but may affect one party more than the other. A telephone line is often clearer in one direction than the other. In some face-to-face situations, such as a theatre box office, one party may be in a relatively quiet office while the other is in an open, noisy environment. Here, there is a particular danger of misunderstanding.

Shyness

Shyness is frequently misunderstood; there are several common misapprehensions. It is sometimes assumed to be a condition that affects only the young. Some think of it as an exclusively female problem. It is often seen as snobbery; the shy person appears 'stuck up'. Shy people are in danger of being regarded as unhelpful, stupid, perhaps gay.

Shy people are not always quiet and retiring; they may compensate in other ways. Some adopt a loud-mouthed, aggressive style. It has been suggested that dictators such as Hitler and Napoleon may have been driven by a need to overcome extreme shyness. Many politicians and actors are naturally shy, in contrast to their public image.

Chronic shyness may be the symptom of other problems, or arise from some change in environment or life-style, such as from rural to urban living. On occasions, it can affect almost anyone. It is worth facing in ourselves and others, and talking about when it occurs. Today, courses are widely available in assertiveness and other approaches that help to overcome shyness.

Fear

Fear can appear the same as shyness, but differs in that it is related to a particular situation or a particular time, and may affect anyone.

It can do much damage to face-to-face communication. At its worst, it can completely stop it; we may freeze or find ourselves unable to utter a word. While this is rare, less serious manifestations are common. We all suffer tenseness, which causes failure to listen, struggling for the right words, saying too little or too much.

Many people experience fear when challenged by a policeman, for example. Most of us feel it when being interviewed for a job. In these and other cases, we often come away feeling we have said the wrong thing, or failed to say the right one.

Related to fear is the problem of uncontrolled speech we call stuttering. This can be a major problem for sufferers. Much can usually be done to combat it, and it is worth seeking professional advice. When faced with someone who has this difficulty, the first need is to recognise the situation quickly, and the second to apply no additional pressure on the sufferer; to do so is like hooting at a learner driver attempting a hill start.

Unfamiliar situations

Most of us develop the skills to communicate, more or less effectively, in the situations we meet every day. But unexpected or unfamiliar situations may find the most articulate at a loss.

We may communicate well with our doctor, in a situation we have faced many times before, but find ourself at a loss for the right words when consulting a solicitor for the first time. If we usually do business in a shop, we could encounter problems trying to sell, for the first time, on the doorstep. Although we converse superbly in the bar on a Saturday evening, we may find ourselves tongue-tied at our first diplomatic reception. A subordinate who communicates well does not necessarily continue to do so when he suddenly finds himself boss.

Practice is always our best friend in such difficulties, but real progress can be made by finding a good role model – someone we can copy – and by taking note of all who give us supportive feedback on our performance.

Face to face – the top 20

The top 10 dos
1. Do think carefully about what you want to achieve before starting any important face-to-face conversation.
2. Do introduce important subjects carefully.
3. Do maintain good but not over-intense eye contact.
4. Do listen actively.
5. Do use humour only with care.
6. Do be aware of and allow for emotional reactions to people and subjects by yourself and others.
7. Do control the speed and loudness of your voice.
8. Do pause often for comment and feedback.
9. Do be aware of body language during conversation.
10. Do listen with attention to what is said.

The top 10 don'ts
1. Don't hesitate too long before broaching important topics.
2. Don't allow preconceptions and biases to get in the way of accurate listening.
3. Don't interrupt unless it is absolutely essential.
4. Don't indulge in long monologues.
5. Don't contradict tactlessly or unnecessarily.
6. Don't change the subject unnecessarily or without warning.
7. Don't look at your watch, out of the window, etc unless you intend to break up a conversation.
8. Don't put words into people's mouths.
9. Don't talk down to people.
10. Don't go on too long.

Chapter 3

Interviews

An 'interview' is a face-to-face discussion in which information is obtained from one person by one or more others. Interviews may be conducted by individuals or by panels. Very occasionally one interviewer may interview several people at the same time. Interviews are used for selection, information gathering, counselling, discipline, selling, interrogation, by reporters, and on radio and TV.

All interviews have many features in common. This chapter is based mainly on selection interviewing, but most of what is discussed can be applied to other types of interview. We will look at the subject first from the point of view of the interviewer, then of the interviewee.

Conducting interviews

To interview effectively, we must get each of the following aspects right:

- preparation
- the introduction
- questioning
- dealing with replies
- the conclusion
- evaluation and action.

Preparation

Interviews are usually planned in advance, whether we are selecting for a job, appraising those who work for us, or obtaining information as part of a consultancy assignment. We must use whatever time we have to prepare carefully, and:

- clarify aims and objectives

- decide whom to interview
- ensure good administration
- prepare ourselves.

Clarifying aims and objectives

We must be clear what our overall aim is and what individual objectives must be met to achieve it. The discipline of writing these down is helpful. For example, we might decide:

1. *Aim:*   To select the most suitable person to fill the vacancy for district sales manager.

   Objectives: — Must be prepared to accept maximum basic salary of £15k.
              — Must be prepared to travel throughout the country whenever necessary.
              — Excellent appearance and presentation.
              — Best relevant experience of our industry and product.
              — Supervisory experience, preferably in a selling context.
              — Articulate and well-spoken.
              — Committed and enthusiastic.

2. *Aim:*   To develop our staff and improve their motivation and commitment.

   Objectives: — Learn how they see their own job performance during the past 12 months.
              — Learn how they see the management and guidance we have given them.
              — Summarise our own perception of their performance.
              — Set objectives for the next period.
              — Identify areas of development need.
              — Agree on an action plan to achieve the necessary development.

3. *Aim:*   To establish the knowledge and personal relationships necessary to sell a consultancy assignment to the XYZ company plc.

   Objectives: — Learn the outline of the XYZ operation.
              — Establish the perceived problem area and the help required.
              — Communicate who we are, how we operate and the way we would approach the assignment.

— Start building a positive relationship with the
XYZ decision-makers.
— Agree the next steps to be taken, when and by
whom.

Deciding whom to interview

The more clearly we have defined our objectives, the easier this will be.

In selection interviews, our objectives enable us to sift the applications received, eliminate those that are clearly unsuitable and build up a short list of those we believe are serious candidates. In conducting a consultancy assignment, our objectives enable us to identify those we need to talk to.

Ensuring good administration

We need to consider the schedule, the place, the travel and reception arrangements, and we may need to set up a panel.

The schedule

To arrange times, we must have a good idea of how long each interview is likely to last. There are several considerations to bear in mind:

- Matters of importance can rarely be explored in less than about 15 minutes.
- The maximum span of attention of even the most practised interviewer and the most willing interviewee is about an hour and a half.
- Time must be allowed after each interview for completion of note-taking, preliminary evaluation, visits to the loo and administrative details.

The place

- Privacy and freedom from interruption and distraction are essential. Our own office can rarely provide this.
- Furniture and the way it is laid out affect the interview. When interviewer and interviewee sit at right angles in low chairs, with perhaps a coffee table in the angle, the atmosphere is very different from an interview in which the two face each other across a large desk. Interviewing across one's own desk in particular creates a feeling of status and a barrier which makes the establishing of rapport harder. If a panel sits in a line at the far side of a table from the candidate the atmosphere is inevitably formal. We should consider our objectives carefully, and experiment with the furniture available.

- For selection interviews, there should be a suitable waiting area for candidates. It should be tidy and comfortable, with reading matter, access to a loo, and the chance of a cup of coffee or tea. Candidates should not be able to overhear other interviews. We should also consider whether we want them to meet other candidates, and if not, make arrangements for this to be avoided.
- Information-gathering interviews are best conducted in the interviewee's normal place of work. This gives the interviewer the opportunity to gain many extra impressions and information.

Travel and reception
If interviewees are travelling we must tell them how to find us, with advice about public transport, a road map and guidance on car parking.

We must make sure that security and reception staff expect interviewees, and are ready to welcome and guide them.

A secretary or someone else on hand can help and comfort, especially if the interviews are running late. Guidance may be welcome with the completion of expense or application forms, or return transport times. If we *are* running late, interviewees should be told, with apologies.

We should decide how interviewees are going to be brought into the interview room. Many interviewers prefer to meet the interviewee outside and conduct him into the room, as this creates a more friendly atmosphere than introduction by a secretary.

Setting up a panel
If the interview is to be conducted by more than one person, the panel will need careful selection and briefing, and should agree in advance how its members will work together. A badly co-ordinated panel has no chance of conducting an effective interview.

Preparing ourselves
We must prepare thoroughly in advance for individual interviews, whatever their purpose, and refresh our memory just before each interview starts.

In advance we must learn as much as we can about each interviewee. To glance at the papers for the first time just before the interview begins is a recipe for disaster. We shall need to study application forms and other sources of information, and decide and note fruitful lines of questioning, gaps in our knowledge and doubts to be resolved. We shall look for common factors in our backgrounds that can help to establish rapport and get the conversation going.

Immediately before the interview we shall glance over the paperwork and the notes we have made to confirm the salient facts: name, where the interviewee comes from, conversational starting points and principal lines of enquiry.

The introduction

At the start of an interview, the objective is to establish a good rapport between interviewee and interviewer as quickly as possible, and to set the scene before moving on to methodical questioning.

Establishing rapport

The aims are to help interviewee and interviewer to relax, and to get the interviewee talking as soon and as freely as possible.

A warm smile and a firm handshake are a good start. We must introduce ourselves and anyone else present, saying enough to explain who everyone is and why they are there, but not burdening the interviewee with information he will not, at this stage, digest.

A friendly enquiry about the journey (if there has been one) is natural, followed by one or two simple and non-threatening questions, for example:

> *'Come in, Mary. We don't seem to have seen much of each other for a couple of weeks. How did your meeting with the chap from the computer department go yesterday?'*

Another approach is to draw attention to some piece of common background such as where both have lived or been educated, common leisure interests, or people both have met. For example:

> *'Hullo, I'm Richard White. I'm the personnel manager; I wrote to you, you may remember. This is Jean Morton, the production director; whoever gets the job will be working with her. I see you used to live in Hereford. I lived there for a couple of years in the seventies. Just where is Malvern Avenue? I can't place it.'*

Sometimes it may reduce tension to get straight to the point; there is no merit in prolonging this phase artificially if the interviewee is ready to proceed. Our knowledge of the interviewee and feeling for his reactions will guide us when to move on.

Setting the scene

Both parties must see the purpose of the interview in the same way. This is the natural time to check what the interviewee already knows, clear up any misunderstandings and provide information that will help him marshal later answers to best advantage. We should also indicate how much time is available and how the interview fits into the overall process. For example:

> *'I think John Smith sent you a letter explaining why I wanted to see you. The marketing director believes the organisation can improve the service it is giving its customers, and has asked me to suggest how this can be done. I am beginning by talking with as many people involved in giving customer service as I can, and learning what they see as the problems and possible solutions. When I have done this, I shall put forward my suggestions as to how service can be improved. This morning, I hope you can spare half an hour to tell me how you fit into the customer service picture, and your feelings about the service you and the rest of the organisation give.'*

Unlike the rest of the interview, the interviewer may do most of the talking during this phase. However, we must not be tempted to go on for too long; interviewees are rarely in a frame of mind to take in much detail. If we have not provided information in advance of the interview, it may be better to feed it in small relevant chunks as we go on.

Simple and carefully explained visual aids can help: organisation charts, job descriptions, appraisal paperwork, product brochures, etc.

Questioning

Information gathering will be the principal objective of almost every interview. To achieve this, we must ask questions, but asking questions is not enough by itself; we must ask them in the context of a sound structure.

Setting the structure

A structure can be devised in several ways. It can be paper-based, sequence-based, objective-based or open-ended:

Paper-based. Appraisal interviews are often based on paperwork completed by interviewee and interviewer before the interview. For example:

> *'In section 1 of the appraisal form you say that you have achieved all the objectives we set last year, but you don't go into detail. There are five objectives listed: could you tell me, briefly, how you feel you met each?'*

Selection interviews may be based on either a CV (curriculum vitae) or a completed application form. For example:

> *'You say you obtained seven GCSEs, but you don't say which or give the grades. What were these, please?'*

However, we must not follow paperwork slavishly. A completed application form, for example, rarely covers the ground we are interested in, giving too much information on some points and too little on others.

Sequence-based. A time sequence can form a good framework. In selection interviewing, many interviewers work through the CV in date order. This provides an excellent structure on which a picture of the interviewee's motivation and personal development can be built up. It also helps the interviewee to remember and the interviewer to check for gaps. For example:

> *'You say here that you left Worldwide plc in 1982. Why did you leave at that time, and why did you choose Littleborough Ltd as your next employers?'*

In information gathering, a process can usually be best understood from a description which follows the sequence in which it is carried out. For example:

> *'You say you handle customer complaints. Suppose I rang up with a complaint: could you tell me, please, exactly what you would do from the moment we first spoke until the matter was finally resolved?'*

Objective-based. Occasionally, the best structure is to work through the list of objectives we have established. However, this may result in a disjointed conversation, and it will certainly make clear to the interviewee what we are looking for – something we may not wish to do.

This approach works better if combined with the time-based approach. We can then expand on phases which appear particularly relevant to our objectives or add supplementary questions after we have followed the time sequence up to date. For example:

> *'That brings us up to date, but I am looking for someone who can demonstrate commitment and enthusiasm. Nothing you have said so far has helped me to judge this in your case. What evidence can you give me that you possess these qualities?'*

Open-ended. Occasionally, it is best to invite the interviewee to suggest a structure. If we have little knowledge of a subject, any implication that we are posing as an expert would cause resentment, and lead to information being taken for granted or deliberately withheld. For example:

> *'Let me be frank from the start. Value engineering is something I have heard of, but know absolutely nothing about. It would help me if you could start by*

explaining what it is and how it works, and then how your own job fits in with the others in the division.'

Asking good questions

This requires much skill. There are several types of question, some of which are useful and some to be avoided. The more useful types are open-ended, closed, yes/no and hypothetical. Those to be avoided include multiple and leading questions.

Open-ended questions offer the interviewee wide scope in framing his answer. They often (but not always) begin with 'Tell me about . . .', 'Why' or 'How'. For example:

'Tell me about your time with Smith and Company.'

'Why have you decided to change jobs?'

'How do you follow up your first letter to sales prospects?'

Such questions are ideal for initial exploration, either of the interviewee as a whole or of specific subjects.

Closed questions call for precise, defined information. They often (but not always) begin with 'Who', 'What', 'When', 'Where', 'Which', 'How much', 'How many', 'How long'. For example:

'Which standard letter do you use if they have not paid on time?'

'How many do you process in the average week?'

Such questions are appropriate whenever facts need to be established. They can often form the basis of a two-stage approach, for example:

'What did you do then?' . . . followed by *'Why did you do that?'*

Yes/no questions are closed questions calling for one of these answers. For example:

'Did you meet your sales target last year?'

Like other closed questions, these will help us to establish facts. However, if used with a tense or inexperienced interviewee, they will do little to get him talking freely. More experienced or relaxed interviewees often help by enlarging on their answer as if they had been asked an open-ended question:

'No, but there were special reasons for that. Two of our main product lines were terminated during the year when the Glasgow factory was closed, and the rise in the pound affected our performance in the North American market.'

Hypothetical questions ask the interviewee to envisage a situation that does not actually exist, to think of an imaginary future or to consider what could have happened in the past. For example:

> *'If the cost of raw material were to double overnight, what course of action would you recommend?'*

> *'If you were in the same situation now, after all your later experience, how would you decide?'*

> *'Suppose you were to get this post, where do you see yourself in five years' time?'*

They are useful for exploring aspects of personality for which the CV offers no evidence.

Multiple questions have two or more parts, for example:

> *'Why did you decide to sell at that time, who advised you, and do you feel you would do the same another time?'*

Such questions are confusing and often presuppose, correctly or otherwise, a particular answer to the first part. They should not be used.

Leading questions are asked in such a way that the interviewer's view and the answer he expects are clearly indicated. They are frequently followed by additional phrases such as ' . . . did you?', ' . . . were you?', . . . could you?' They often start with a phrase such as 'I don't suppose . . .', 'I don't expect . . .', 'I don't imagine . . .' For example:

> *'You didn't allow him to get away with that, did you?'*

> *'I don't suppose you believed her?'*

Closed questions can be made into leading questions by the tone of voice. For example:

> *'And that was the last you heard of it?'*

Such questions do not help. They make it clear what the interviewer expects and wishes to hear, and are unlikely to produce additional information. They should not be used.

Dealing with replies

It is not enough to ask good questions. We must also:

- listen
- evaluate

- modify our approach
- take notes.

Listening

There are a number of aids to effective listening:

Active listening involves the use of appropriate gestures and noises of encouragement such as smiles, nods and grunts. Words interjected at the right moment will have the same effect: 'I see', 'Really!', 'Go on', 'Right', 'Yes', etc.

We must avoid actions which discourage a reply; glancing at a watch or out of the window, doodling, noticing a distraction, losing eye contact at a critical juncture, etc.

Occasionally, the need will not be to encourage but to hold back an over-talkative interviewee. In such circumstances, the opposite tactics should be used.

Avoiding preconceptions is essential for effective listening. If we think we know what the speaker is about to say, not only do we fail to listen, but we may be convinced we have heard something that was not said. Interviewers with strong preconceptions about a subject or about the interviewee may have serious listening problems.

The *body language* of both interviewer and interviewee can aid the listening process. The interviewer can use body language to encourage and stimulate a response. He can lean forward, adopt an alert posture, and use facial expression to encourage and respond to what is being said.

By observing the body language of the interviewee, the interviewer can add to his understanding of the replies. Small movements of the hands, narrowing or opening of the eyes, eye contact or lack of it and facial expression may suggest tension, doubt, disagreement, dislike or the reverse.

'Hearing between the lines' is similar to the way in which we should read testimonials; what is *not* said can be more important than what *is* said. Interviewees will naturally play down or ignore aspects of any possible answer they think may be unfavourable to them, while making much of those aspects they believe to be favourable. The effective interviewer will be alert to such manoeuvres, noting not only what is said, but also what might have been said but was not. For example:

> *'Were your proposals implemented?'*
> *'My report was very well received. The chairman himself congratulated me,*

and the management committee fully accepted my approach and set up a working party.'
'Were they implemented?'
'No.'

Summary and restatement by the interviewer of what he believes the interviewee has said is a useful way of checking that he has heard and understood correctly. For example:

> *'So, if I hear you correctly, you feel that the period you spent with Smith and Co was of value in your personal development, but that towards the end you were being exploited, and the company was not able to use your abilities and knowledge to the full?'*

Evaluation

Evaluation is important in all types of interview. Complete evaluation of the replies can usually only be made after an interview has finished. If it is one of a series, we need to compare the claims of each interviewee systematically (this process is discussed on page 56).

However, we will also need to make a running evaluation of each reply which will affect how we conduct the remainder of the interview. We can decide to probe or challenge a reply, ask for it to be expanded, follow up a completely new line, or abort a subject we were intending to explore.

Evaluation involves judging the credibility and completeness of the reply, the interviewee's motivation in giving it, and its bearing on other aspects of what we need to know.

Once in a while an interviewee may make a 'career stopping' remark, which cannot satisfactorily be modified or withdrawn, and which fundamentally changes our view of the person or the situation. However, these are very rare; normally, each reply will need to be built into and interpreted as part of the overall impression.

Replies need to be compared during the course of the interview to ensure consistency. For example:

> *'I'm sorry, but if I heard you correctly a few minutes ago, you were saying that these reports were never revealed to a third party. What you have just said suggests to me that they may be shown to staff in other departments if they have a query. Can you enlighten me as to which is correct?'*

The halo effect. It is vital to restrain what some writers describe as the 'halo effect'; that is, the tendency to judge – even to hear – what an interviewee says later in the light of one or two early favourable or unfavourable replies.

An interviewee may, for example, have a good Oxbridge degree, or perhaps a first-rate record in another field. But our satisfaction at these may prevent us from giving full weight to his clearly unsatisfactory job performance during the past few years.

Reactions

We are engaging in a dialogue, and our reactions to what we are told depend on the style of interview we have chosen. Some interviewers deliberately create a barrier between themselves and the interviewee. They conduct one-way questioning, refusing to respond to questions or react to statements by the interviewee. Other interviewers regard an interview as a 'conversation with a purpose', and respond and react in a more natural way.

Whatever style we adopt, it is best to hide strongly favourable or unfavourable reactions, as these would affect what the interviewee chose to tell us subsequently.

Note-taking

Taking notes is essential to effective interviewing. It is impossible to remember everything that happens during an interview of any length. If the interview is one of a series, the scope for confusion is even greater. Without good records, interviewees will be confused with one another, and memory of them and what they have said will become a blur.

But the peril is even greater than this. Memory is highly selective. Interviewers tend to form a judgement about an interviewee within the first one or two minutes. Hence, if notes are not taken, we remember what reinforces our judgement, and forget what does not. This is one of the principal reasons that, in unskilled hands, interviewing can be such a poor selection tool.

However, these problems must be overcome, as the penalties for not taking notes are too high. A number of techniques can help us:

The folding clipboard. A clipboard with a folding cover keeps the notes confidential both during and at the end of the interview. The clipboard can be held up, making it impossible for the interviewee to read what is being written, and easier for the interviewer to maintain eye contact. The pocket in the facing cover of the clipboard can be used to hold papers, such as the applicant's CV or application form.

Asking permission. If we feel the need, we can ask the interviewee's permission to take notes, or at least politely indicate that we intend to do so. Interviewees never object; most feel mildly flattered that their words are being noted for posterity.

Preparation. The page of blank notepaper should be already headed with the date, the names of all present, and any other reference heading before the interview starts. Apart from saving time, this will act as a crib. It is worth developing your personal shorthand, abbreviating whenever possible.

Short cuts. In fact-finding interviews, it is worth checking if any of the necessary information (the organisation structure of a department, for example, or a work procedure) is available in documentary form.

Delay. The noting of sensitive points should be delayed until the interviewee is talking about something else. If, in particular, he makes some damaging admission, it is best to wait until he is answering a later question, to avoid drawing his attention to the note. This is also best for favourable replies, or the interviewer risks being inundated with much more of the same kind.

Use quotes. Difficult though it may be, we must try to note particularly important replies verbatim, so that we have them on record for later interpretation.

Using these and similar techniques, we will develop the skill of noting what we need to remember, quietly and in many cases without the interviewee being aware of it.

The conclusion

The objectives of this phase are:

- answering the interviewee's questions
- giving an opportunity to make final statements
- explaining what will happen next
- final farewells.

Answering the interviewee's questions

Information should have been provided to the interviewee before the interview, during the introduction, and as necessary during the main discussion. However, it is important, especially in selection interviews, to give a clear opportunity towards the end for the interviewee to ask questions, and we must allow sufficient time for this in the schedule. For example:

> *'Are there any aspects of the post you are still not clear about, or any other questions you would like to ask me?'*

'Yes, I'm not clear what my budgetary responsibility would be; when would I need to seek approval, and what would be within my own authority?'

The kind of questions asked can often give us further information about the way a candidate's mind is working and what he considers important. For example:

'Only the question of relocation. I had been hoping it would have been acceptable to work from my present home, but I would like your confirmation of this.'

Giving an opportunity to make final statements

The interviewee must be given the chance to correct any wrong impressions he feels he may have created, or make any points he has not found the chance to make. For example:

'Is there anything we haven't given you the chance to say, or any other points you would like us to bear in mind?'

Explaining what will happen next

As in any normal social situation, we will aim to draw smoothly and courteously to a close, dropping appropriate hints before we do so to avoid an impression of rudeness. This will be made easier if, in the scene-setting phase, we indicated the time available.

The interviewee should be clear what will happen next, and when it is likely to happen. For example:

'Well, thank you for all the information you have given me, which is extremely useful. I must go away now and digest it carefully. My plan is to submit a report to the directorate by the end of the month, and I would like to let you see a draft of the section covering your operation. I hope you won't mind if I contact you again if I discover anything else I need to know.'

Final farewells

In selection interviews, it is important to say nothing that could be interpreted as a comment on how the interview has gone or the view we have formed of the candidate. Even a cheery 'See you again, I hope!' will be misinterpreted.

With very tense candidates, the feeling that the final whistle has blown can help them to talk freely for the first time. They may say something as they are conducted out of the room, in the lift, or during the farewells, that gives us information we have failed to get during the interview. Should this happen, continuation in the foyer, a car to the station, or perhaps even in a cafe down the road, may be of great value.

Evaluation and action

If the interview has achieved its objectives, there will be several important tasks to complete afterwards. These are likely to include:

- post-mortem and writing up
- final evaluation
- action.

Post-mortem and writing up

After any interview we need to collect our thoughts, and, if it was conducted by more than one person, to exchange impressions and information. Despite the notes taken during the interview, we may need to complete writing up our impressions while the memory is fresh. There may be an interview record or other formal documentation to be completed.

Final evaluation

With a series of interviews, it will not be possible to complete our evaluation until the end. This is particularly true of selection interviews, where the temptation to judge candidates as we go along is strong. The feeling that we have found what we are looking for in the first interview is not only unfair to later candidates, but can also affect the way we treat them and listen to their replies. We may become blind to the even better candidate we meet later.

The same applies to premature rejection of a candidate's claims. If we do this, we may fail to realise that he is the best on the list, and with slightly more open-minded treatment could have proved himself to our satisfaction.

In fact-finding interviews, later interviews may affect the way we evaluate what we have learnt earlier. As we proceed, we build up a perspective which can indicate that we need to know more about subjects we dismissed earlier, or possibly challenge what we have been told.

The problems of evaluation can be particularly difficult if there is more than one interviewer. Panels often fail through having no clear method of working either during the interview or when evaluating, and discussions can be unsystematic and ruined by interpersonal tensions.

Panels will usually be more effective and time will be saved if they discuss and agree what process to use before attempting the evaluation itself. If there are interpersonal tensions, it is best to talk these through rather than let them harm the evaluation process. The worst problems tend to arise when the panel is chaired by an over-dominant or opinionated senior member.

It is helpful to agree what criteria are being used for evaluation before discussion of any individual candidate. A matrix can be set up, preferably on a flipchart, on which evaluation of candidates can be made systematically. Some criteria may be 'musts' – no candidate can be considered further unless he meets them. Such 'musts' must be measurable. The remaining criteria will be 'wants'; these can be weighted and candidates scored against each. If this is done, the total of a candidate's scores will give a preliminary indication of the panel's choice. For example:

		Candidate 1	Candidate 2	Candidate 3	Candidate 4
MUST					
Be prepared to accept £15k basic salary		✓	✓	✓	✓
Be prepared to travel throughout UK		✓	✓	✓	X
WANT	*Weight*				
Good appearance & presentation	10	8/80	10/100	7/70	—
Experience of industry & production	9	10/90	6/54	10/90	—
Supervisory experience	8	10/80	0/0	3/24	—
Articulate & well-spoken	8	6/48	10/80	8/64	—
Committed & enthusiastic	5	7/35	10/50	9/45	—
		333	284	293	-

The evaluation process, whether by a panel or an individual, should be completed by asking the question 'If we choose this candidate, *what might go wrong?*' In this way, unexpected factors or unexplored doubts are thrown up, which could suggest revision of the preliminary choice, follow up of references, checking of qualifications, or even a further interview.

Action

No series of interviews is complete until whatever has been decided has actually happened.

With selection interviews, this involves ensuring that successful and unsuccessful candidates are notified. It is, however, unwise to send rejections until the chosen candidate has confirmed acceptance. This is no time for administrative delays; good candidates move fast, and we may need to exert pressure on other individuals or departments involved.

With appraisal interviews, certain actions, such as fulfilling training needs, job rotation or restructuring, and performance monitoring, were probably agreed. If they do not happen as planned, the whole process may fall into disrepute.

With fact-finding interviews, there will usually be recommendations to frame, a report to write and present and, above all, the need to ensure implementation of our recommendations.

Conducting interviews – the top 20

The top 10 dos
1. Do read all paperwork well in advance.
2. Do look for common background to help establish rapport.
3. Do explain the procedure.
4. Do ask open questions, especially early on.
5. Do listen to replies with care – right to the end.
6. Do probe gaps and unsatisfactory replies thoroughly.
7. Do take plenty of notes during the interview.
8. Do delay noting sensitive replies.
9. Do give adequate opportunity for the interviewee to ask questions.
10. Do make clear what the next steps are.

The top 10 don'ts
1. Don't leave personal preparation until the last minute.
2. Don't make premature judgements.
3. Don't allow purely personal biases to affect judgement.
4. Don't ask tricky questions early on.
5. Don't talk too much.
6. Don't ask leading questions.
7. Don't ask multiple questions.
8. Don't interrupt or put words into an interviewee's mouth.
9. Don't show strongly favourable or unfavourable reactions.
10. Don't suffer the 'halo effect'.

Being interviewed

A few people shine at interview, even to the extent of landing jobs for which they are unsuited. Most of us, however, await being interviewed with trepidation but, as with other activities, we can do a lot to improve our performance. The previous section of this chapter, on conducting an interview, gives an insight into the likely approach of recruiters. Here are some guidelines for us when we are a candidate.

As a candidate for interview, we should:

Before the interview – Research the organisation and the job – Check how we match up – Consider the likely interview format – Anticipate questions – Dress the part – Plan the logistics – Think success.

At the interview – Start well – Weigh up the interviewers – Listen carefully – Reply skilfully – Ask good questions – Finish on a top note.

Before the interview

Research the organisation and the job
We must know as much as possible about the post we have applied for and the organisation offering it. We need to know what the purpose of the post is, its main duties, and the location. Other aspects, such as reporting relationships, remuneration package, opportunities for train-ing and advancement and hours of work, can be explored at the interview. We should research what the organisation does, its owner-ship (public or private, part of a group of independent, UK or other nationality owned), its size, history, financial soundness and manage-ment culture. We should not hesitate to ask the recruiters for any information they can let us have; this will help to confirm our serious interest in the post. Other sources of information include:

- the advertisement (if there is one)
- directories and other reference books or databases
- our own personal contacts.

As a last hope, recruiters often leave annual reports, sales literature and house magazines in the interview waiting room.

Check how we match up
If we are keen to get a job – we may be unemployed – there is the temptation to apply for posts which do not match what we have to

offer. But rejection always brings discouragement; even worse, if we are accepted, such a job is unlikely to lead to happiness and success.

A systematic analysis is essential. We must match our skills, experience, interests and objectives, and an honest assessment of our weaknesses, failures and dislikes, against what the job could provide.

Consider the likely interview format

Interview methods vary. A common pattern for senior posts is a first, in-depth interview, often on a one-to-one basis. This may be conducted by a consultant or experienced member of the personnel department, and often takes the form of methodical exploration of our CV. For short-listed candidates, there may be shorter panel interviews conducted by senior individuals to assess how well the candidate's personality will blend with those they would work with and with the culture of the organisation.

Most interviews, especially by experienced interviewers, are conducted in a friendly, open way. 'Stress interviews', in which candidates are deliberately embarrassed or put under undue pressure, are rare. Psychometric tests may be incorporated in the selection procedure. Candidates may be given the chance to see the operation and to meet other staff.

Anticipate questions

It is usually possible to anticipate and prepare for most of the questions we may be asked. They are likely to explore:

- education, training and qualifications
- work history and experience
- specialist knowledge
- responsibilities held
- motivation and ambitions
- our successes, failures and achievements.

If there are aspects about which we are unhappy (for example, a period of unemployment, a failed exam, a disagreement with an employer), we should plan how best to present our case. It can be helpful to rehearse replies on key points, preferably in front of a discerning friend.

Dress the part

We should appear at interview smartly and appropriately dressed, but there can be a danger of over-dressing. We should decide how the holder of the job should be dressed, and go just one stage better.

Naturally, we must pay attention to the finer details of turnout; hair, shoes, finger nails and so on. We may sense the need to use a breath freshener. Too much scent or aftershave and extremes of colour of pattern in clothes must be avoided.

Plan the logistics

Nothing is worse than arriving late, breathless and flushed. We must allow plenty of time for the journey. If it is convenient, public transport may be relaxing, but we must allow for lateness. If we drive, we should check the car-parking situation, and whether we need to pre-book or obtain authority. We will need to allow for delays, and perhaps for walking from a remote car park; in a large organisation, even crossing a factory or office complex from front gate to interview room can take time.

We may decide to take a portfolio with examples of our work, but they must be relevant and easy to look at during interview.

A clipboard on which to note information given during interview and containing prompt notes, will, if not over-used, appear efficient and can help to reduce nerves.

Think success

A positive frame of mind is essential for success at interview as in other competitive activities. A review of our strengths and the reminder that we have the internal resources to cope are a good starting point. Beyond this there are many personal approaches. Some people find it helpful to picture the sensations of a successful interview vividly, just as some athletes picture the sensations of a record performance. Others may have some talisman – a piece of jewellery, or clothing perhaps – which gives them confidence.

At the interview

Start well

We must be on our guard from the first contact. Car-park attendants, commissionaires, security guards, secretaries and other staff will all form an impression of us, and may give input to the decision.

Virtually everyone feels nervous before an interview. However, provided they are not extreme, nerves help by setting the adrenalin flowing and preparing us for peak performance. If we are too relaxed, we are unlikely to shine.

Once in the interview room, it is crucial to get off to a good start. Candidates are judged within the first one or two minutes of an interview. Inexperienced interviewers (and we will meet many of those) may judge us by nothing more than how we walk across the room, the strength of our handshake or how we sit down. We must therefore enter confidently but not brashly, with a pleasant smile, respond to an offered handshake firmly, wait until we are invited to sit, and remain quiet but alert to the opening moves by the interviewer.

Weigh up the interviewers

Inexperienced interviewers are likely to be at least as nervous as the candidate. While we must not under any circumstances patronise or dominate, there will often be ways in which we can tactfully make the task easier for them.

Just as the interviewers will be trying to find out how good the 'chemistry' is between us, so we should do the same from our side; few jobs are worth having if we do not get on well with our boss.

Listen carefully

Many mistakes arise from failure to understand, or even to hear properly, questions or statements by the interviewer. We may hear what we expect to hear rather than what is actually said. It is good practice to pause for a few seconds before starting a response to all but the simplest of questions. This will give us time to reflect, and will be seen as a compliment to the interviewer's wisdom. If we remain in doubt, it is better to check, by repeating or paraphrasing the question or asking for it to be repeated, than to risk an inappropriate answer.

We should always try to assess what is in the interviewer's mind, and the reasoning behind each question. The order in which questions, particularly supplementary and probing ones, are asked will often provide a clue.

Reply skilfully

The answers we give to the interviewer's questions are, inevitably, the crux of the interview. Apart from listening to the words', good interviewers will watch our unspoken reactions and body language: posture, gestures and facial expression. Our aim must be to convey a sense of relaxed alertness, and avoid indications of tension.

In general, our answers should:

- Address both the point raised and what we believe to be the reason for it being raised
- Be well structured and logical, beginning with a clear statement, which is then explained or enlarged on

- Be neither too long nor too short. Brief answers should be reserved for simple, purely factual questions, but we must also know when to stop.
- Be spoken clearly, confidently, naturally and with good but not obsessive eye contact.

We must be prepared to be asked about a subject from different angles; we must not be so tied to the words used by the interviewer that we fail to make our case. While blatant evasion is sure to be spotted, we should take every reasonable opportunity to draw the discussion on to our own ground.

Attempts at bluffing will always be spotted by experienced interviewers, and risk disaster; it is much wiser to keep within the bounds of our knowledge. We should also never depart from the path of truth; were we to get the job, serious misstatements could lead to dismissal.

Ask good questions

Good interviewers – especially consultants, who often play the role of honest broker between candidate and employer – will offer chances for us to fill gaps in our knowledge of the post and the organisation. We should be ready to make full use of these, and plan two or three questions to ask. It is much better if these are not confined to 'pay and rations' details.

Finish on a top note

The second most important phase of every interview is the conclusion. Good interviewers will give the opportunity for us to clear any outstanding questions or make any final points before we leave. Even if they do not, we should ensure we do so; few feelings are worse than leaving an interview thinking 'If only they had asked me such-and-such a question!' However, we must not repeat points we have already made, go on too long, or press our case too insistently.

We should leave the interview room as we arrived, confidently but not brashly, shaking hands firmly and with a friendly smile.

There is a danger of relaxing too soon. The interviewer or a colleague may conduct us to the door or beyond. There is a temptation to say something incautious if we feel the pressure is off, but anything we do (or don't do) may legitimately be used in evidence!

Being interviewed – the top 20

The top 10 dos
1. Research organisation and job thoroughly.
2. Anticipate likely questions.
3. Dress the part.
4. Plan the logistics.
5. Get off to a good start.
6. Weigh up the interviewers.
7. Listen with care.
8. Reply confidently but not brashly.
9. Ask good questions.
10. Think success throughout.

The top 10 don'ts
1. Apply for unsuitable jobs.
2. Over-dress.
3. Risk arriving late.
4. Be rude to secretaries, receptionists or other staff.
5. Assume the interviewers are skilled and confident.
6. Offer a flabby handshake.
7. Answer until you are sure you understand the question.
8. Give very short or very long answers.
9. Attempt bluffing or deceit.
10. Let down you guard too soon.

Chapter 4

Oral Presentation

The term 'public speaking' covers an enormous range of activities, from a major speech to an audience of thousands with TV cameras and the world's press watching every move, to a meeting of half a dozen colleagues in an office or even a sitting-room. Between these extremes come sales presentations, talks to clubs and other leisure organisations, after-dinner speaking, political meetings, teaching, preaching, addressing a court and many others.

The steps to success in each are similar. We must:

- profile occasion, audience and location
- define aim and objectives
- gather material
- structure the presentation
- choose aids and methods
- produce speaker's notes
- rehearse
- present
- deal with questions.

Each of these is now considered.

Profiling occasion, audience and location

More presentations go wrong through lack of this analysis than for any other reason. To complete our profile, we must ask questions about the occasion, the audience and the location.

At first sight, audience analysis in advance may appear difficult, but in many situations it is possible to anticipate the characteristics of our audience quite accurately.

To get answers, we can talk initially to the people who invited us to speak. They will want success as much as we do, and will usually help as much as they can, although they can be over-optimistic, especially about the number of people expected.

We may know one or two people who plan to be present, and can sound out their expectations. If the event is a regular one, we should be able to find people who have attended previously.

Whatever our sources, we must add cool thought and common sense. We could waste weeks of effort in research, only to be confronted by absolute beginners; prepare visual aids suitable for an audience of hundreds, only to find three men and a dog; or prepare a speech to rally the faithful, only to find ourselves confronted by a room of implacable opponents.

If there is an opportunity to see the room in advance, it will be worth taking. We can see at first hand its size, shape and facilities, and perhaps relieve the tension of the Big Day, by making it into familiar territory.

A suggested checklist for profiling occasion, audience and location is given on page 88.

Defining aim and objectives

Having completed the profile, we are in a position to set an overall aim and define the objectives necessary to achieve it. We may want, for example, to inform, train, persuade, obtain action, sell, amuse, enliven, negotiate or any combination of these.

The subject itself requires careful thought. What is the centre of our message, what are its boundaries and what is outside its scope? What has already been covered in previous presentations or documents?

It is useful to define objectives from the audience's point of view rather than our own. We should write statements such as: 'After the presentation, participants will: know . . ., understand . . ., be able to . . ., accept that . . ., be ready to . . . etc.'

For example, if we have been asked to give a presentation to a monthly meeting of colleagues from other departments in our organisation, we might define our aim and objectives:

Aim: To make clear how the work of the Marketing Department supports that of the other departments represented.

Objectives: After the presentation, participants will:
— know what the Marketing Department does
— understand how it helps their work
— accept the importance of its role
— have expressed any problems they have with working relationships with our department.

Gathering material

If the subject is topical, we have been asked to make a study specially, or have agreed to talk on a subject we are not familiar with, we may need to prepare from scratch. On the other hand, we may have material already at our fingertips, because we handle it every day or are expert in the subject.

Starting from scratch

Sources of material. We are rarely on our own when gathering material. Within organisations there are often individuals, records, literature or perhaps departments that can help us. Outside, the resources of libraries are immense, and the staff invariably well-informed and helpful.

Research can be further helped by electronic means. A worldwide network of databases covers many subjects, and equipment, in the form of a micro and a modem, can give access to such databases directly from work or home. Otherwise, most good public libraries, among other sources, will give advice and help.

Apart from subject matter, there are many books which provide stories, humour and approaches specifically for the public speaker.

Prepare in good time. There is much to be said for preparing well in advance; the mind works best when it has time to digest material. Preparation just before a speech is not as satisfactory as the same work done weeks earlier. If we have sufficient time, we will become comfortable and familiar with the material and integrate it into our thinking. We will also have the chance to pick up additional material in the interim.

Personal experience. Audiences, however distinguished or sophisticated, do not like too many dry facts or too much abstract reasoning; they all respond to human interest and personal experience. Stories and illustrations from real life, and especially from our own experience, are the most valuable material of all. They stamp the presentation with our personality, and provided they are carefully chosen and well presented, will attract and hold attention.

The amount of material. It is always useful to prepare more material than we expect to use. By going the 'extra mile', we give ourselves confidence, and will be well placed to answer questions and contribute during discussion. It is dangerous and uncomfortable to speak from the utmost limit of one's knowledge.

However, the fear of not having enough often leads inexperienced speakers to provide too much. For every speech that runs short of material there are many more that contain too much.

Reviewing old material

It is dangerous to pull old notes off the shelf just before a presentation and expect them to see us through. We must review them carefully, however many times we have used them previously. Indeed, in many ways, the more often we have used our material, the greater the dangers.

The dangers of old material. If we have used the same material many times, we may have become bored with it. There could be gaps because events have moved on since we last used it. Our previous audiences may have had different expectations or levels of expertise. We may not have taken account of lessons or facts we learnt during previous presentations. The material may not have worked well the last time we used it.

Adapting material. Particular care must be taken if we are basing our presentation on a report or article. Reports usually contain more material than should be used in a presentation, are too packed with facts and figures, and may not be in the best order for a live audience.

Structuring the presentation

The need for structure

A clear, explicit structure is essential; we must give our audience every aid to listening and understanding that we can. It may develop as we are gathering our material, or we may need to construct it as a separate step, but it must exist. There are several reasons for this:

The attention span of audiences is very short. Depending on how it is defined and how stringently it is measured, it can be said to stretch from a couple of minutes to a maximum of about 20; it is certainly less than speakers believe.

Attention follows a curve; it builds up rapidly (if the speaker is succeeding) at the start. For a while, it continues to build up further but more slowly, and then starts to decline, slowly at first, but with increasing speed. This pattern is true not only for the whole presentation, but also for individual sections within it, *provided* they are clearly signposted. Thus a good structure may help us to retain or even increase attention during a speech.

Other audience problems. Even with good structure, the amount of material an audience can cope with is limited. Not only the attention, but the understanding and memory of an audience are far less than speakers like to believe.

When reading, people can go back to pick up points they have missed, forgotten or failed to understand. They can lay the book aside and think it over, refer to other sources and come back to it. None of this is possible during a speech. The audience must take it in as it is delivered or not at all.

An experiment. To demonstrate the difficulty, try to write down the material covered during the last presentation you attended. Better still, if the opportunity ever arises, give a speech yourself and then (without advance warning) ask the audience to write down all they can remember. The results will be very humbling.

Planning a structure

A basic approach. Some of the oldest advice on structuring a speech is:

> *'First you tell them what you're going to tell them. Next, you tell them. Then you tell them what you've told them.'*

This simplest of structures emphasises the need for a clear introduction, a simple message, and a good conclusion.

The main points. We must limit both the number of points we make and the amount of material within each. In general, between three and six main points is the most any presentation should contain. For optimum understanding and retention, the complete list must be introduced at the start, and each separate point introduced, structured and summarised.

The order. The order of the points must be easy to follow. There is usually a logical thread that will guide us. We may be describing a process or events in a time sequence. If in doubt how to place two points, we should ask 'Will the audience understand that before I have told them about this?' If there is no other method of choosing an order, we should move from the simpler to the more complicated.

A storyline or narrative structure can be effective, as it carries the attention forward in a natural flow. Narrative structure can rarely be used for a complete presentation, but may often be suitable for individual sections, frequently in the form of a case study.

Shaping the material

Straightforward material. It may become clear that what we want to say falls easily into a suitable number of linked points or headings.

For example, for the Marketing Department presentation mentioned on page 66, the structure might be:

1. Introduction
2. The mission of our department
3. The organisation structure and the people
4. The way it works with other departments
5. Some problems we experience
6. Conclusion

Subheadings. We shall work by allocating material appropriately to each main heading.

As we do this, we are likely to realise the need for subheadings. The rules are the same as for main headings: there should be no more than about five under any main heading, and the order should be logical and easy to follow. If we do create subheadings, we must not produce an overall structure that is too complex or overloaded.

For example, we may develop section 3 of the departmental presentation:

3 – Organisation structure and people
As already described (section 2), the departmental mission has three parts:
- *Each part is the responsibility of a separate section, each with a section head reporting to the departmental manager*
- *The sections are:*
  - □ *advertising (Tony Greaves)*
  - □ *market research (Mary Hodgson)*
  - □ *product development (Karen Moore).*
- *Tony has two people; Fred and Anne. They both do the same sort of work.*
- *Mary does not have any helpers.*
- *Karen has six people; Joan, Arthur, Michael, Sharon, Peter and Katherine. Joan and Arthur work together on the latest product range; the rest have one model from the old range each.*
- *Everyone has contact with other departments, which I will tell you about now.*

For some headings, a narrative approach, perhaps based on a case study, may be chosen. For example, we could base section 5 of the Marketing Department presentation, 'Some problems we experience', on a typical example or case study.

Checking each heading. We must examine each heading, asking:

- Is it linked to the previous heading?
- Is the subject clearly defined or introduced?
- Is the development logical?
- Are any subheadings necessary and in the best order?
- Is it supported and explained by sufficient, suitable facts, figures, quotations, etc?
- Is it linked to the next heading?

Difficult material. Occasionally, material may prove difficult to divide into a suitable number of headings. The most common problem is to have too many.

If we are lucky, this problem may disappear as we digest our material and come to understand it better; freshly gained knowledge often appears as a lot of separate trees rather than a clearly shaped wood. If familiarity does not bring simplification, we must eliminate less important points, or make some into subheadings under a principal heading.

Choosing aids and methods

Whatever the type of speech or presentation, we should consider using visual aids.

The value of visual aids

Visual aids:

- attract and hold attention
- help understanding
- reinforce the message.

Attract and hold attention. Just as most people look first at the pictures in a new book, so most members of an audience are spontaneously interested by visual aids. They awaken those who are dozing and focus minds that are getting hazy.

Help understanding. To say that 'one picture is worth a thousand words' is to understate the case. In many situations, an audience would switch off long before the thousandth word, and never reach the insight that one picture would have brought instantaneously.

Many concepts are difficult to explain in words. Try, for example, describing a spiral staircase to someone who has never seen one. With the aid of a picture, however, the nature of the thing becomes immediately clear.

The same is true of sizes and spatial relationships; in words, they may be virtually impossible to describe, but with maps, plans or diagrams they will be communicated at once. For example, in the Marketing Department presentation, section 4 – the way it works with other departments – will be far better expressed by a diagram than in words:

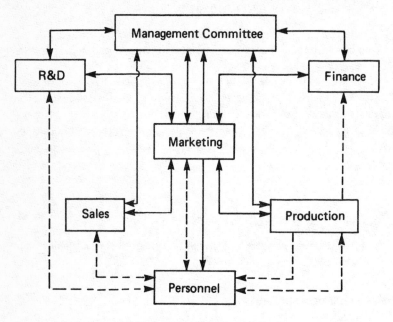

Inter-departmental communication

The presentation of figures, particularly statistics, cries out for graphs and charts. For example, section 5 of the presentation – Some problems we experience – might include data on complaints about a particular product. Rather than a verbal description, a pie chart would help.

Some presenters use pictograms to express relationships and abstract concepts. Complex ideas can be reduced to arrangements of simple geometric shapes; triangles, circles, thick and thin lines, etc. Section 2 of the presentation – The mission of our department – would benefit from a pictogram illustrating the product life-cycle. This approach can be helpful, but is easily overdone, and unless the pictograms are really appropriate they can hinder rather than help.

Pie chart

Reinforce the message. By using an additional sense – sight – visual aids open another gate into the participants' minds. A message that is presented both orally and visually has a better chance than one which is only presented orally. For this reason, many speakers use overhead projector foils or slides listing headings or key words for each point they wish to make.

By convention, aids are rarely used for formal speeches, but understanding and retention will benefit in any kind of speech.

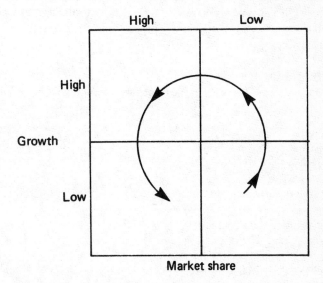

The product life-cycle

Common aids
The most common and useful aids include:

- blackboard and chalk
- prepared flipcharts
- blank flipcharts
- overhead projector and foils
- films and videotapes
- slides
- tape/slide projectors
- models
- samples
- handouts.

Models and samples are particularly useful, as they involve yet another sense. Touch and handling can be of tremendous value. We could, for example, talk for many minutes about the nature of a material without communicating a fraction of what could be achieved by a moment's handling.

Choose simple aids. The complexity and cost of the visual aids available becomes ever greater. However, for most uses, simple aids are best. Complex aids draw attention towards themselves away from the speaker and his message, and are more likely to go wrong.

Skilled use. All aids, simple or complex, require skilled use. It is essential to practise with any aid we do not know well. Learning to set up and use the more complex aids may need professional help. Some tips are suggested on page 84.

The environment
The wrong choice of room can ruin a presentation. If the choice is ours, we must consider:

- size
- heating and ventilation
- lighting
- noise levels
- distractions
- equipment
- furniture
- positioning.

If possible, we should inspect the room beforehand to familiarise ourselves with it, and to discuss any potential problems with those

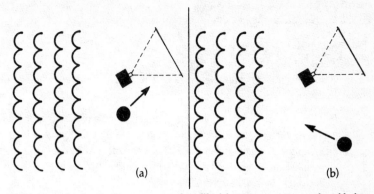

In (b) the speaker has good eye contact and, unlike (a), is not competing with or blocking sight of the visual aid

responsible. There may be adjustments we can make, such as rearranging furniture or speaking from a particular position.

Producing speaker's notes

Good speaker's notes are the best protection against speaker's nerves, and for this reason alone are essential.

Too many or too few? Inexperienced speakers often make one of two mistakes: too many notes or too few.

A few speakers can spellbind an audience without a single note, but this is not a sensible model to follow. The vast majority of first-rate speakers use notes; it makes their job far easier, and is fully accepted by an audience.

On the other hand, some inexperienced speakers write out their script in full and read it verbatim. However, few can write a script that sounds natural, and even fewer can read naturally. We cannot maintain eye contact with our audience while reading, nor can we adjust a script to meet unexpected situations.

A good format for notes. Good notes should have clear headings for each main section, followed by subheadings (if they are used) listed in order. Under each, we should add a brief summary of the point and essential facts, figures or examples. The notes should include simple coded references to any visual aids we plan to use.

If we have structured our presentation systematically, as described earlier, the speaker's notes will be a simple adaptation of the structure we have already produced.

For example, speaker's notes for section 2 of the Marketing Department presentation – the mission of our department – would be:

2 – The Marketing Department's mission
— Show VA 1 — the mission statement;
The mission of the Marketing Department is to aid the financial health of the organisation by:

- *knowing relevant economic, technological, social and political developments*
- *analysing the opportunities and threats presented by market and products*
- *knowing the strengths and weaknesses of competitors*
- *using media to best advantage for the organisation*
- *maintaining necessary statistics*
  read & explain
- *show VA 2 – diagram of product life-cycle from dogs through problem children and stars to cash cows [see above]; explain*
- *the three basic strands; advertising, market research and individual product support*
  explain.

Some experienced speakers write each main section on a separate card; this helps to emphasise the structure to both speaker and audience. Cards should be numbered and tied loosely together in one corner to keep them in order even if dropped.

An alternative to notes is a 'mind map'.* A speaker asked to give a talk on Iceland drew a map and wrote around it all the words he associated with that country. He then sorted these into groups, colour coded with a highlighter. The finished plan for his talk looked like this:

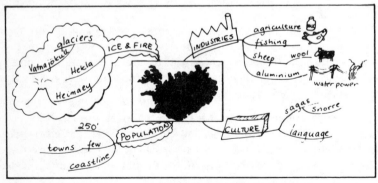

A mind map for a talk on Iceland
(© Ingemar Svantesson)

* *Mind Mapping and Memory*, Ingemar Svantesson, Kogan Page, 1989.

Using visual aids as notes. If we have decided to summarise all our points on overhead foils or slides, it may be practicable to use these as our notes. However, if we do so we must keep a copy available in case the project fails or the VAs are lost.

The teleprompt. The teleprompt or autocue is a device which unrolls a script before our eyes unseen to the audience. However, it requires a specially produced script, a machine, an operator and at least one rehearsal in the room to be used, things we are unlikely to have. Even if we did, the result is usually more wooden than a presentation given from good notes.

Rehearsing

We should rehearse any new or important speech or presentation. Team presentations in particular always need rehearsal, to ensure coordination between team members.

If possible, we should rehearse in front of an audience, even if only of one person. Ideally, they should be typical of the participants we expect to address. If this is not possible, we should brief them carefully on the occasion and the expected audience. To be helpful, our rehearsal audience must be honest and prepared to be critical; people on either side of a boss–subordinate relationship may find this difficult.

Rehearsing can be more nerve-racking than giving the speech itself, but will only help if we take it seriously. We must say what we actually intend to say, and not skip passages or become self-conscious. We should certainly rehearse with the aids we plan to use. Ideally, the rehearsal should be in the room where the speech is to be given; check that aids are visible from the back.

We should check the timing during rehearsal, although rehearsals seldom take as long as delivery to a live audience, and can be up to 25 per cent quicker.

A video with camera is an immense help; to see and hear ourselves is the best lesson of all. Failing this, we may be able to achieve something with a mirror or an audio recorder.

It is possible to over-rehearse. We must not allow ourselves to go on to the point where we lose spontaneity and become slick, or even lose interest in what we are saying.

Presenting

It is no accident that we have been so long coming to the event itself. If we have prepared thoroughly, we will be able to face the occasion with quiet confidence.

The points important to success are:

- control of nerves
- overall mood
- the start
- use of the voice
- use of the body
- eye contact
- use of aids
- the conclusion.

Control of nerves

All speakers suffer nerves. Public speaking probably causes more anxiety than any other activity ordinary people have to undertake.

There is a number of remedies, although the perfect solution for one speaker may offer no help to another. The following tips have helped speakers to cope with nerves; one may be right for us.

Nerves are beneficial. We must accept that nerves in moderation are beneficial. Nerves set the adrenalin flowing and ensure that body and mind are geared to give of their best. Nearly all practised performers, whether actors, singers, instrumentalists or speakers, suffer from nerves before they come on. It is when we feel no nerves at all that our speech is more likely to fall flat.

Use good notes. The value of good notes as protection against nerves has already been mentioned, and can hardly be over-emphasised.

Visualise success. Many athletes picture themselves achieving success immediately before they undertake a competitive activity. Long jumpers, for example, while they stand ready to start, will imagine every detail of the sensation of making a record jump, from their first steps down the track to the rapturous cheers of the crowd.

Some speakers find the same mental process reduces their anxiety before speaking, and vividly imagine themselves making a successful speech just before they begin.

Rationalise. It can help to define clearly what we fear.

The most common fear is of *drying up*. But if we have prepared carefully and provided ourselves with good notes, this is unlikely. There is nothing wrong with an occasional pause to collect our thoughts or find the place in our notes; it helps the audience to reflect on the wise things we have said. We have no obligation to maintain a continuous torrent of words; as Wagner said in only a slightly different context, 'The most beautiful thing in music is silence.'

A related fear is *not finding the right word*. This also is unlikely with good preparation, and matters far less than we think. Speakers, unlike writers, are not expected always to find the *mot juste*. They have the opportunity to experiment with several. Indeed, what is a wrong word for one member of the audience may be perfect for another. If there are points in our presentation where we feel a word or phrase may elude us, we should spell them out verbatim in our notes.

Another common fear is *making a fool of oneself*. Exactly what might happen is usually not specified. But unless we have upset them in some extraordinary way (such as being gratuitously rude about them, their organisation or their beliefs – things that no sane speaker would ever do) the audience will want us to succeed, and help us to do so.

If a speaker or performer does appear to be in serious difficulty, the embarrassment is at least as keen for audience as for performer. For this reason, audiences will almost always do what they can to avoid such embarrassment. If we have established an easy, friendly relationship with them, they will suggest words, wait politely while we collect our thoughts, even offer helpful questions. The best possible advice is, quite simply, not to flap.

They probably won't notice. It is surprising but true that nervousness felt by a speaker often goes unnoticed by his audience. It is hard enough to guess what is in someone else's mind at the best of times; at the other end of a crowded room in poor light the chances are even less. This provides a further reason for avoiding a show of panic.

Relaxation. Some speakers benefit from using relaxation techniques before they start: deep breathing, or even yoga or a hot bath, if they are available, will help.

Sharp objects. At least one expert advises holding some sharp object so tightly that it hurts. Suitable objects might be a bunch of keys or the sides of the lectern. The idea is that the slight pain provides a focus for our anxieties, freeing us from other fears.

Picture them in the nude. Anything which helps us to realise that we and our audience are all human beings can reduce unnecessary nerves. To imagine the audience unclothed helps some speakers to do this.

Overall mood

As speaker, it will be our responsibility to set the overall mood of the presentation. The mood we want will depend on our objectives, the occasion and the audience, but some ingredients are necessary for virtually every speech:

Professionalism is a must. To ask an audience to give us its full time and attention is no small matter. We can only expect it if we can demonstrate that we are worth listening to; that what we have to say and the way we say it are worthy of respect.

The right degree of formality. Our analysis of the occasion and the audience should tell us how formal our speech should be. Unless there are clear indications otherwise, it is best to aim at an informal but not familiar style. We should try to establish a rapport, as near to a simple one-to-one relationship as we can.

Empathy and audience contact. Whatever the degree of formality, we must make and keep contact with our audience. To help us do this, we should observe faces and maintain regular eye contact with as many as practicable. We should be aware of mood and reactions as conveyed by facial expression, shuffling feet, glancing at watches, rustling of papers or frequent shifting of position.

Depending on the nature of the presentation, some speakers like to test audience reaction at critical junctures: can they hear, do they follow, are they in agreement? The simplest method is usually to ask directly.

Controlled enthusiasm. The mood we generate will almost always benefit from an injection of controlled enthusiasm. The aim must be to communicate our interest and enthusiasm for what we have to say, using tone of voice, pace of delivery, facial expression and appropriate gestures.

It is, of course, possible to be too gushing and enthusiastic; few things are more wearing. But for most speakers this is much less likely than the danger of appearing too slow, tentative and boring, especially during a long presentation.

Pace and drive without hurry. It is up to us to keep things moving forward purposefully, especially if the audience has just eaten, or towards the end of a tiring day. Undue hurry must be avoided, but we must provide sufficient pace and drive.

The start
This is the most important phase of every presentation. We need to gain the full attention of the audience right away, as it will be difficult to gain later. Like the take-off of an aircraft, we need to apply full power at once.

There are several time-honoured ways of gaining audience attention: telling a funny story, making a provocative statement, showing a key visual aid, or doing something unusual and arresting.

Funny stories are the most common device. They have the double advantage of helping to establish empathy with the audience as well as gaining their attention.

However, for success, we must choose a story that is funny, tell it well, and demonstrate a valid link between the story and our subject. If the link is lacking, we achieve little and have to start a second time gaining attention for our subject – something which may be harder than if we had not opened with the joke.

We must take care that our story cannot offend – audiences are sensitive until they have learnt to trust a speaker. If in doubt, we should play safe and try a different opening.

Provocative statements may be effective, and act like headlines in drawing the audience's attention to a key aspect of our message without telling the full story. For our marketing presentation, we might consider alternatives such as:

'Marketing is the oldest management activity in the world.'

'Some people think the Marketing Department is a waste of time and money; we are certain it is the most important in the company.'

'It has been said there are liars, damned liars and marketing departments. I want to prove to you that this is quite true.'

The art of headline writing is to pick out the centre of a story and encapsulate it, in an intriguing and witty way. Those who have this art should use it to enliven the start of their speeches.

A more flat-footed but still effective approach is to pick out one of the most remarkable or unexpected conclusions from our material and begin by stating it baldly and without explanation. If we are successful, the audience will want to learn how the statement can be justified. For example, we could try:

'One of the worst mistakes anyone can make is to call a member of the Marketing Department "a salesperson".'

A visual aid can form an excellent start, particularly if we produce one specially for the task; bright, interesting and simple. As with all other forms of opening, it must be relevant to our message.

The skill with which it is used is as important as the aid itself. We can produce it immediately, even dramatically, and allow the audience to study it for a few moments in silence, or give only the barest explanation initially and return to it at a later stage.

An unusual and arresting action, if we can think of one, may be effective. We may produce and manipulate some object relevant to our subject, appear dressed in or carrying relevant clothing or equipment, or mime an action or sequence.

Such openings can be effective and memorable, provided they are relevant, and provided we are able to carry them through with the necessary touch of drama.

Never apologise. We must avoid starting with remarks which might suggest that we are not worth listening to. We must believe that what we have to say will justify the audience's time and attention, and communicate this conviction from the start.

Use of the voice
If the audience cannot hear what we have to say, all else is wasted.

Acoustics. The acoustics of rooms vary, both because of the room itself, and according to the number of people present and where they are sitting. If we have the slightest doubt whether we can be heard, we should ask our audience.

If the acoustics are bad, we must speak more slowly and loudly; basic audibility is essential, and the refinements can come later. Such an extreme situation may occur when addressing an open air meeting.

The conventional glass of water can help in voice production, lubricating a dry throat and lowering the pitch noticeably.

Microphones. Sound-enhancing equipment is now widely available; if it is there, we should use it, but it should be used properly.

With a stand mike we must ensure that we speak within the optimum pick-up range, and our movements will be limited. Some stand mikes can, however, be detached from the stand and hand-held, and we should check before we start. A hand-held mike, or one with a tie or necklace mounting, is more satisfactory than a stand microphone. It allows us to turn away to look, for example, at visual aids. If it has a long lead or a radio link, we can move around freely.

Many microphones have a sliding switch on the stem, although trembling fingers can have difficulty in locating it. We should use the simple tap-test before speaking, but not so loudly as to deafen our audience.

Speed, variety and meaning. The aim should be to 'put a shine in our voice';

to sound switched-on, lively and enthusiastic. We must listen to ourselves, and be aware of what we are trying to say, so that the meaning shines through.

We must pace our delivery with care. The basic speed must be right: neither too fast nor too slow. An honest friend will advise us.

Having got the basic speed right, we must learn to vary it intelligently, to avoid monotony and reinforce the meaning. Regular, rhythmical variation is the most sleep-producing of all. To emphasise a point and give our audience time to catch up, we should also use occasional pauses; used at the right time, silence is a powerful technique. Here also, the glass of water can help; the business of sipping from it provides a reason for an acceptable pause while we collect our thoughts.

Use of the body
We are conscious of our body when addressing an audience. We have to decide where to place it and what to do with our hands and feet, and it has a tendency to get in the way.

Sit or stand? It is usually best to stand when addressing even a small audience. This makes it easier to see and be seen and heard; makes us more alert; and indicates respect for our audience and the importance of what we are doing.

The only exception might be when leading a group discussion with a very small audience. Sitting, possibly on the front of the speaker's table, suggests maximum informality and invites group participation.

Stand easily. We should stand as naturally as possible, with weight balanced evenly. Gripping the sides of the lectern loosely looks natural, and is convenient for our hands.

Placing our notes. It is awkward and distracting to speaker and audience to hold notes throughout a speech. Eye contact with the audience is also easier if notes are not too far from eye level. If there is a lectern, we can use that. Otherwise we can improvise one from boxes, files or books.

We should plan in advance where to keep notes in relation to visual aids, and how to move when using them. If, for example, we are using an overhead projector, we will need to minimise the to-ing and fro-ing between projector and podium.

Avoid distracting mannerisms. Nerves may cause movements which are distracting to the audience, such as fiddling with markers, pencils or glasses, placing hands in the pockets, swaying from side to side or pacing to and fro.

This is not to suggest we should stand stock still, but we must avoid unnatural, strained or repetitive movements.

Gestures. It is probably safest to avoid the use of gestures at first, unless we are sure of our skill. There is a danger of falling into repetitive and meaningless gestures which become a distraction and give an impression of weakness.

As we develop confidence and experience it will become easier to judge how to use gesture to best effect. This is an area in which video recording is particularly valuable.

Smile. P G Wodehouse said, 'Mere exercise of the risible muscles has been proved to be beneficial.' We may not feel like smiling, but we should try. Participants will usually smile back, and the whole mood will be lightened.

Eye contact

We should establish and maintain eye contact with as many members of our audience as possible. This helps to establish rapport, gain attention, and acts as a real channel for feedback and reaction.

There is a danger of biased eye contact, perhaps towards someone who we find particularly responsive (there is at least one in every audience), someone who is sitting at a convenient angle, or an attractive member of the opposite sex. We should make a conscious effort to look round the whole group.

We must avoid negative eye use, such as glancing out of the window or at our watch. If no clock is visible some speakers take their watches off and place them beside their notes at the start of the presentation.

Use of aids

Having chosen our aids, it is essential to use them well. This should be done smoothly and unobtrusively, so that the audience is not aware of the aid, only of the message it conveys.

Do not split attention. Whatever aid we are using, it is vital not to split the audience's attention. This happens if, for example, we pass round a handout and continue to talk. The audience will start to read the handout, thus missing what we are saying.

The same occurs if we display a complete slide or viewfoil while talking about one point on it only. The audience reads ahead of us, missing what we are trying to tell them about the first item. It is better to hide points we have not yet reached with a sheet of paper and reveal them one by one when we are ready.

To avoid distraction, we should always remove an aid we have finished with, unless we need to return to it frequently.

Attend to detail. Small details can make a big difference to the overall effect.

When using a blank flipchart (or a blackboard), we should write *before* we speak the key words, so attention is focused on what we are doing. If we speak the words first and then write them, attention is lost while we write. We should always write from the side, so the words are visible to the audience as we write, and also write large enough to be read comfortably from the back of the room.

If we are using an overhead projector, it is better to turn it off when we are not using it, especially if it has a noisy fan.

Avoid too many words. We must avoid slides and viewfoils with too many words. They should normally carry only one or two short, simple sentences or a list of single key words.

Better still, we should use pictures, graphs, charts and diagrams as much as possible, for the reasons mentioned earlier in this chapter.

Don't be a slave to your aids. Aids should always remain 'aids'. If they are too complex, intrusive or demanding, we lose our audience to the aid. Simple, well-used aids – flipcharts, viewfoils or slides – are best for most presentations.

The conclusion

The end of a speech is only second in importance to the beginning. It is the part that has the best chance of remaining in the hearers' memories, and will thus have a disproportionate impact on how they judge us and what we have said. A fine conclusion can lift a mediocre presentation into a higher class.

Not with a whimper but a bang. Good endings may include a challenge to action, a question, or a punchy summary of what we have said. They provide the opportunity, not to add new material, but to drive home the points we have already made.

Rehearse. Whatever else we rehearse, we should make sure we have practised both start and finish.

Dealing with questions

This is not necessarily the same as 'answering questions'; sometimes it is best not to attempt an answer. There are a number of alternatives:

- throw the question to a colleague
- throw the question to the audience
- throw the question back to the questioner
- admit ignorance (and say we will find out)
- postpone an answer until later in the presentation
- give clues that will help the questioner to develop his own answer
- answer a different question
- waffle meaninglessly
- refuse to answer (with or without an excuse)
- carry on as if we haven't heard
- turn the situation into a joke
- walk out
- feign illness or death.

While some of these may be too extreme for normal use, and all are only appropriate for specific circumstances, we should never forget their existence. Many politicians have survived on them for years.

Anticipation

We must do all we can, especially when analysing our expected audience, to anticipate likely questions or objections. If we know something of the interests, expertise or hobby-horses of those present, we know that some of what we have to say will cause doubt, disbelief or controversy.

As suggested earlier, we should always prepare material over and above what we plan to use in our presentation. Apart from the additional confidence and reserve in case of shortage that this provides, it helps when answering questions.

If we have established a rapport with our audience, maintained good eye contact and read the mood correctly, we will realise as we speak if something has not gone down well. Tomatoes are rarely thrown in these days of high prices, but shuffling feet or an exchange of significant glances may suggest problems to come.

Guide the audience

If we have a Chair, it will be his duty to guide the audience on when and how questions will be taken. If we do not, we must give this guidance ourselves. Questions can be taken at several points.

We can suggest that people feel free to *interrupt* with questions or comments as we go along. This is best for informal presentations, when objectives will include participation and feedback, and for training sessions. It can help in other situations too, as feedback may suggest a change of plans to meet the audience's needs.

We can plan *pauses for questions* or clarification at the end of each main section. This is especially helpful during a long presentation or lecture, and when one of our main objectives is the transfer of knowledge.

We can indicate that we would prefer questions to be kept *until we have finished speaking*. This is usual for more formal speeches and the presentation of papers, and allows us to develop our thesis fully.

Of course, even if guidance has been given, and certainly if it has not, members of the audience may choose to interrupt, heckle, disagree, or to correct what they believe to be an error or misrepresentation. We will usually get warning of this, but it may be very short. If we are on controversial ground, we cannot afford to relax.

When questions come

Listen carefully to what is actually said, right to the end. There is always the danger of listening only to the start, and thus failing to grasp what is really being asked. This applies particularly if we are anxious about possible hostile questions; it is easy to assume a questioner is being critical when he is actually being supportive.

Repeat. Repetition is legitimate if everyone did not hear the original question (eg if it was asked from the front row), to eliminate misunderstanding, or, provided it is not too obvious, to play for time. We can repeat the exact words, to check we have heard, or paraphrase, to check we have understood.

Be courteous. However we feel inside, we should indicate our appreciation that the questioner has taken the trouble to explore our thinking. We should thank the questioner explicitly for his question, say that he has raised an interesting point, or simply smile and use some turn of phrase to convey appreciation.

We should adopt this approach even if we believe the question is particularly stupid, or has been fully covered in what we have just said. If we do, the rest of the audience will be on our side; if we do not, they are likely to side with the questioner. It is amazing what interest and hidden significance we can find behind a silly question if we really try, especially if it comes from an influential member of the audience.

Separate. Multi-part questions are often asked, and it is always best to disentangle them and answer each part separately, choosing the easiest first.

Beware of assumptions. It is possible, particularly when involved in controversy, to be drawn into accepting an assumption without realising. Always review the assumptions behind a question before attempting an answer, and if necessary challenge them politely but firmly.

Keep cool. If aggressive or personal questions *are* asked (and this will be much rarer than we fear) then coolness under fire is essential. It is often possible to ignore unpleasant innuendos, while still answering the main question. A touch of humour can defuse many situations, if we have the gift for it. Sarcasm, however, must never be used.

Admit ignorance. If we know our subject (and we are unlikely to be speaking if we do not) there should be few occasions on which we will not be able to give a factual answer. However, if we are caught out, the only sensible strategy is to admit ignorance immediately and with as little embarrassment as possible, to say we will find out, and to keep the promise.

Occasionally, for example if there is an acknowledged expert in the audience, it will be appropriate to ask for help. If we have established a good audience relationship, this is likely to be forthcoming.

Time answers. Good answers are usually neither too long nor too short. If an answer appears simple and short, it may be courteous and helpful to expand it with appropriate background.

On the other hand, we should not go on too long, or use a question as an opportunity to throw in irrelevant material we forgot to use in our speech.

Use other strategies. The many alternatives to answering a question directly were listed at the start of this section, on pages 85–6.

Presentation profile checklist

The occasion
- What organisation is holding it?
- Has it: any special mission?
           any special procedures or rituals?
- What kind of occasion is it?
- Timing: when will I start?
           for how long?
           is this flexible or fixed?

- Will there be:
                    questions?
                    discussion?
  If so, for how long?
- Will there be a Chair for my presentation?
  If so: who?
                what does he know about me?
                when will we meet?
- Are there to be other speakers?
  If so: how many?
                who?
                are they before or after me?
                what are their subjects?
- Will I participate in a panel discussion?
  If so: when?
                on what subject?
                with whom?

The audience
- How many are expected?
- Why will they be there?
- Will they be representatives or there in their own right?
- How knowledgeable will they be?
- Will they have preconceptions or biases?
  If so, what?
- Will they be unusually friendly or hostile?
  If so, why?
- Might there be tensions within the audience?
  If so, what and between whom?
- Who will be the key figures?

The location
- Is the setting formal or informal?
- Is there a platform?
- Will there be a lectern?
- What are the acoustics like?
- Will there be public address equipment?
  If so, what kind of microphone?
- Visual aids:
  what will be available?
  who will control their operation?
  how?

Oral presentation – the top 20

The top 10 dos
1. Do check what is expected of you when invited to speak.
2. Do prepare in plenty of time.
3. Do establish a clear structure for the speech.
4. Do prepare good, summarised speaker's notes.
5. Do realise and accept that all good speakers experience nervous tension before speaking.
6. Do plan and rehearse the start with care.
7. Do put pace and enthusiasm into your delivery.
8. Do ensure you are clearly audible to everyone, asking if in doubt.
9. Do maintain good, evenly distributed eye contact with your audience.
10. Do plan and rehearse the conclusion with care.

The top 10 don'ts
1. Don't prepare too much material; check timing in rehearsal.
2. Don't try to do without speaker's notes.
3. Don't read a verbatim script.
4. Don't start with any sort of apology.
5. Don't risk weak or dodgy jokes.
6. Don't split your audience's attention by misuse of visual aids or handouts.
7. Don't rock, sway or use repetitive gestures.
8. Don't use visual aids with too many words on them.
9. Don't gabble or rush your delivery.
10. Don't assume your audience is hostile, especially at question time.

Chapter 5

Meetings

An effective meeting is a highly efficient tool of communication, not only in our working lives, but also in our leisure activities. Sadly, not every meeting is effective.

Whether our role is chairing a meeting, acting as secretary or participating, a methodical approach will greatly improve our effectiveness. Such an approach should include:

- planning
- personal preparation
- effective chairing
- effective secretaryship
- effective participation
- good follow-up.

Planning

The ingredients of a well-planned meeting are:

- deciding whether a meeting is necessary
- setting objectives
- producing the agenda
- choosing who should be present
- choosing time and place, and notifying participants.

Deciding whether a meeting is necessary
This is the $64,000 question.

Well-run meetings are a highly efficient way, sometimes the only way, of decision-making, group communication, generating ideas, negotiating, and helping to build a team. In some circumstances, there may be legal reasons for holding a meeting.

On the other hand, unnecessary or badly run meetings do much harm. They waste time, stimulate disagreement and tension, cause unnecessary expense and produce unrepresentative decisions.

Calling a meeting can be a soft option or a way of avoiding responsibility – we dare not decide on our own, so we call a meeting. Some meetings are called to give an excuse for delay, others to persuade the powers that be that action is being taken. Others are called to bolster the self-importance of the Chair, and give him the opportunity to parade his opinions and power.

Regular meetings – every week, month or whatever – can be the worst culprits. It takes courage to cancel a regular meeting. But, as Professor Northcote Parkinson has pointed out, 'work expands to fill the time available for its completion'. Nothing is easier than filling the agenda of a regular meeting.

In deciding whether a meeting is necessary, we should always consider the alternatives. Would it be better to make the decision ourselves, to communicate in writing or by telephone, or perhaps to postpone action until the situation has become clearer?

Setting objectives

Defining objectives is *not* the same as producing the agenda. An agenda is a list of subjects to be covered; objectives are what we wish to achieve in those subjects and for the meeting as a whole. The agenda for a business meeting might be:

> 1. Apologies
>
> 2. Notes of last meeting
>
> 3. Departmental records
>
> 4. Budget position
>
> 5. Ideas for new products
>
> 6. Any other business
>
> 7. Date of next meeting

Invalid objectives. Looking at objectives for each heading, we might find that items 1, 2 and 7 only have a purpose *if* the meeting is called regularly. Items 3 and 4 would be covered during the normal process of management – there is nothing to be gained by discussion in a meeting. Item 5 is unlikely to lead to anything of value. Item 6 is a make-weight; if anything of importance is to be discussed it should be specified.

Valid objectives. On the other hand, examining our objectives for the same agenda, we might find:

Item 3 has the objective of communicating the current plans and activities to all, so that any overlaps, inconsistencies or omissions can be rectified. It may also stimulate comparisons between departmental performance, thus motivating departmental managers to higher achievement.

Item 4 has the objective of communicating a major change in the annual budget imposed by the management committee, and discussing the actions the division and its managers will have to take to meet the new criteria.

Item 5 has the objective of generating at least six new ideas, one of which can replace a product which is about to be withdrawn.

None of these objectives is reflected in the wording of the agenda; a better wording will be discussed under the next heading.

Formal or informal? The degree of formality with which we plan to conduct the meeting will depend on the nature of the group and of the business. If, for example, our objective is creativity, we should plan for maximum informality. If, on the other hand, the meeting has legal status, such as a company annual general meeting, we should be scrupulously formal.

Producing the agenda

A meeting will be far more effective if those attending know in advance what is to be discussed. They will then be able to sort out their ideas, gather data, sound out the views of colleagues, and come well informed and ready to contribute.

These advantages are so obvious, it is difficult to understand why this is one of the most frequently ignored aspects of meeting preparation. The reason may be that some managers regard a meeting as an opportunity to conduct a viva voce examination of their subordinates. In doing so, they inevitably reduce the overall effectiveness of their meetings.

When producing the agenda, certain standard items are usually included:

Any *apologies for absence* are usually mentioned and noted before the start of business.

If the meeting is one of a series, *approval of the minutes* or notes of the previous meeting will be needed. At formal and semi-formal meetings, the Chair will then sign the minutes.

Any *matters arising* from the minutes, *which are not somewhere else* on the agenda can then be raised.

Other items of business can now be listed. The order may depend on importance (with the most important early on), or possibly when certain people are likely to join or leave the meeting. Some people prefer to put routine items (correspondence received by the Secretary, routine reports, etc) early on, in order to get them out of the way.

If anyone entitled to attend the meeting asks for a legitimate item to be included, it is always best to include it.

It is usual to put an item *any other business* near the end of the agenda. However, this can lead to discussion of business members have not been notified about and for which they are unprepared, often when they are tired and anxious to get away. To prevent this, the Chair may call for items participants wish to raise under 'Any other business' to be notified at the *start* of the meeting. This will help to limit the risk and give members time to think about them.

The concluding item, if the meeting is one of a series, is *date of next meeting*. This is a good idea, as arranging a date with all concerned present can usually be done in a minute, but afterwards may take several days of phone calls.

A good agenda will not just list the titles of items, but will indicate what each should achieve. It may also indicate who is to lead the discussion or, in formal meetings, who is to propose a motion. It will be supported by copies of any papers or reports necessary. For example:

Agenda

1. *Apologies for absence*

2. *Notes of meeting of 12/6/90*

3. *Departmental reports*
    All heads of department to highlight major aspects
    (Reports attached)

4. *Budget position*
    Director to report on management committee review. Meeting to consider implications for the division
    (Copy of MC Minute 149 attached)

5. *New products*
    Discussion of possible replacements for the 109 range, led by J Smith, Marketing

6. *Any other business*
    (To be notified at the start of business)

7. *Date of next meeting*

Choosing who should be present

In general, the smaller the meeting, the better; it will be easier to control, and participants will have a better chance of contributing fully.

For some meetings, there can be no doubt who should be invited; all subscribing members, for example, all heads of department, or all shareholders. Other meetings may present problems. We have to perform a balancing act between those who can really contribute and those who will be offended if not invited.

Choosing time and place, and notifying participants

For a series of meetings, it is best to fix dates as far in advance as possible. At the least, the date of the next meeting should be fixed at the one before.

A poor room can lead to a poor meeting. The place should provide good facilities for the size and kind of meeting to be held. It should be neither much too big nor much too small, as free from visual or aural distractions as possible, warm but well ventilated, suitably furnished, and neither too formal nor too casual. If travel is involved, the location should be easy to find, have good car parking, and be accessible by public transport.

The boss's office is probably not a good place, as it is liable to interruption by phone or visitor and the atmosphere is often laden with status.

As well as notification, agenda and supporting papers should be sent as far in advance as possible. The notification has a special importance for formal meetings, as it should provide assurance that all entitled have the chance to be present, and there are often rules about how, when and to whom notification must be sent. In the most formal meetings, the first act may be to read out the calling notice, thus enabling anyone to challenge its validity and placing it on the record.

Personal preparation

Good preparation is a main key to effective meetings. Chair, Secretary and participants must all prepare.

The Chair must prepare himself at least as well as other participants. Apart from the subject matter, he must consider strategy; he should think of the personalities, politics and interests involved, and try to anticipate how the discussion will evolve, what alliances and disagreements will arise, and where problems may lurk.

The Secretary will need to satisfy himself that all has been made ready. He should have with him a formidable array of equipment, including spare copies of the agenda, supporting papers and previous minutes, plenty of notepaper, flipcharts, stapler or paper clips, and assorted writing implements. He will need a list of those invited and the files of relevant correspondence, and possibly a register or signing-in book, receipt book, membership cards, place cards or badges. If the meeting is formal or semi-formal, he will need a copy of the standing orders, rule-book or bylaws which control its proceedings.

The Secretary should be the first to arrive in the meeting room. If it is in a hotel, pub or conference centre he must make contact with the staff to ensure that meal breaks, message-taking and reception arrangements are understood.

Room layout. The Secretary should always ensure that the room is laid out properly in whatever style is appropriate for the size, degree of participation and formality of the meeting.

The way furniture is arranged for meetings can have a big effect on their atmosphere and efficiency. For example, a meeting held round a boardroom table has a completely different atmosphere from one in which participants are free to place their chairs where they wish.

One writer has distinguished over 30 different arrangements, although the distinctions between some are rather fine. Common arrangements include:

- boardroom
- round table
- negotiating
- freestyle
- theatre style
- schoolroom
- horseshoe
- herring-bone.

Members of smaller, participative meetings will usually be seated round one large table (or several tables or desks placed together) in boardroom layout. If, however, there is to be a presentation, the horseshoe or hollow-U arrangement, in which a separate table with necessary visual aids is placed at one end of the room, may be better.

For larger meetings, the choice usually lies between theatre style, in which members sit in rows facing a top table at which speakers and office holders sit, and schoolroom, which is similar but with desks or tables for participants. Schoolroom is most appropriate when partici-

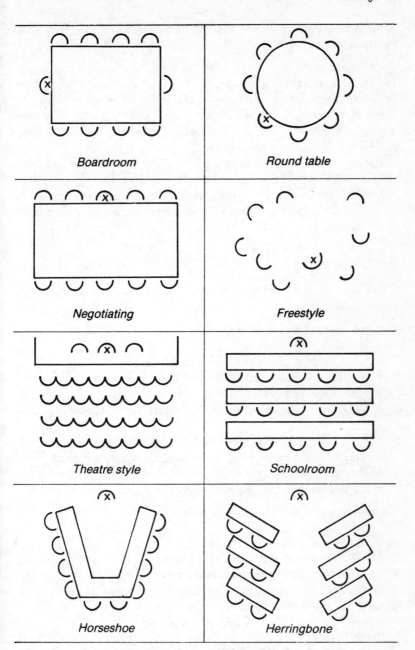

Seating arrangements for meetings (X = Chair)

pants have a lot of paperwork or writing, or if the room would look empty with chairs only.

Participants are always ready to blame the Chair for a poor meeting, but are often themselves responsible through lack of preparation. It is, of course, essential that participants should be given every chance to prepare. Handing out major reports and other documents at the meeting itself makes sensible discussion impossible, and participants can refuse to accept such treatment.

Having received their papers in advance, it is the participants' responsibility to read and digest them, not on the train to the meeting, not just as the item is being introduced, but sufficiently far ahead to read, mark, understand, and complete any necessary research or consultation.

Effective chairing

The Chair will make or break the meeting by the way he conducts it. It is his responsibility to:

- set the tone and style of the meeting
- establish clear objectives
- focus its thinking on the various subjects
- ensure all present contribute their best
- control the verbose and ill-tempered
- safeguard the rules by which the meeting or its parent organisation operates
- maintain order and safety for all present
- ensure that clear, acceptable conclusions are reached on all items
- observe timekeeping
- see to arrangements for the comfort of participants.

Guidelines to help in these tasks include:

Arrive in good time
This will help to establish leadership from the start, and enable the Chair to meet and evaluate newcomers, as well as holding any preliminary discussions with individuals or on points that might cause difficulty in the meeting itself.

Consider seating
Where people sit can affect the feel of a meeting and its efficiency (see page 96). The Chair who wishes to control this should use place cards to indicate where he would like people to sit.

Start on time
It is businesslike and courteous to those who have arrived on time to start promptly. Occasionally, there are special circumstances which justify delaying the start, such as key participants held up by a late train, but these should be rare.

Start as you mean to go on
The Chair must set the atmosphere and style he wants right at the start: brisk, businesslike but friendly, and anything else the objectives require.

Clear away the chores
Notices about car parking and transport, message-taking arrangements, catering, smoking, break and finishing times and so on, are usually best dealt with right at the start.

The Chair should then turn to any personal matters; introduction of newcomers, congratulations, condolences and good wishes for members or former members, and apologies for non-attendance. Finally, he should seek approval of any previous minutes or notes as a correct record.

Matters arising
The discussion of matters arising from the notes of a previous meeting is the first point of possible difficulty. This should normally be a quick item, confined to reporting on agreed actions that have (or have not) been taken, and which are *not* elsewhere on the agenda. Anything else should be ruled out of order.

Visual aids
Visual aids can be a great help in controlling a meeting. By noting points on a blank flipchart, the Chair can avoid backtracking and repetition, aid clarity, reduce the heat of debate, aid memory and understanding, and form the basis of the subsequent record.

Shaping the discussion
Discussion usually passes through four phases: introduction, delineation, debate and decision. The Chair must know what stage the discussion has reached, and help participants to understand as well.

Introduction. In this phase, attention must be gained and focused on the subject at issue. In a formal meeting, each item of business will be in the form of a motion introduced by a proposer. In less formal meetings, it is helpful for each item to be introduced by a subject leader. The Chair may do this, but if so, he should keep his own views hidden at least until the discussion is well under way.

Delineation. During this phase, participants with clear views will state them, and other participants will grasp what issues are to be decided.

Debate. This is the main phase, during which opinions will be formed and firmed up, alliances made and differences clarified. It will continue until material, time or possibly the participants are exhausted.

Decision. The Chair will need to spot the point at which it is right to press for a decision. To do so too soon will result in a poor decision and discontented participants. To do so too late will waste time, fray tempers and may also result in a poor decision.

Disciplined debate

One or two rules apply to virtually every meeting, however formal or informal. They include obedience to the Chair, speaking only when invited by the Chair, sticking to the subject, debating 'through the Chair', and interrupting only for procedural reasons. It is the participants' duty to obey these rules, and the Chair's to ensure they are obeyed. The Chair must avoid heavy-handedness, but will command support in enforcing these rules for the benefit of all, and must not hesitate to do so. More meetings are damaged by weak chairing than by firm, clear direction.

Using the resources of participants

To work properly, meetings must use the knowledge and skills of their participants to best effect. The Chair must therefore know or quickly learn about the strong points of those present. He must encourage newcomers and the nervous, while restraining the opinionated and verbose.

He should listen carefully to what is being said, even after lunch. He must try, as far as possible, to conduct the debate like a game of tennis, calling on speakers from opposite points of view alternately. Above all he must be scrupulously fair in giving a hearing to all points of view, even those with which he disagrees.

He should only express his own views in the later stages of a debate in which no one else has expressed them.

Good manners and humour

Participants will need to remain well mannered, however hard-fought and important the issues. The Chair must set an example in this. An occasional touch of humour can help to cool tempers, although too much humour from the Chair quickly palls.

Clock-watching

The Chair should never lose sight of time, and when necessary should be firm but polite in drawing attention to its passing. After a certain point, the longer debate goes on the less fruitful it becomes. If it is clear that an important subject cannot be resolved in the time available, the Chair should suggest adjournment to another occasion.

Creativity and criticism

Most discussions include putting forward ideas, and criticism of them. Discussions do not go well if both processes are allowed to happen at the same time. Typically, one speaker makes a suggestion, a second disagrees, and others then line up behind the two points of view, leading to a lengthy and possibly acrimonious debate. But while this goes on, the best idea may not even have been expressed. Less forceful participants may not put forward their ideas if unrestrained criticism is allowed throughout a debate.

If, however, the Chair calls for ideas before allowing criticism, then there is a greater chance that everyone's ideas will be heard. If they are listed on a flipchart, the process becomes even easier: some can clearly be ruled out, others will be seen as worth consideration, and balanced debate on the remainder is assured.

Decision-making

The ideal method of decision-making is universal consensus. The Chair must quickly spot whether this can be achieved before any participant is tempted to generate differences for the sake of it.

Formal and informal meetings tend to approach decisions from opposite directions. In formal meetings, debate can only take place if a motion has been proposed and seconded. In informal meetings, there may be doubt or even confusion as to what decision is being suggested. The more formal approach is often better, and the Chair of an informal meeting should get a form of words written down, preferably on a visual aid, as the point of decision is approached.

If consensus is not possible, there are four options:

1. *Imposed decision*. The Chair can, having listened to the discussion, impose an arbitrary decision. This makes sense only if he holds authority over those in the meeting, as manager of a department, perhaps, or chairman of a society.

2. *Adjournment.* The discussion can be adjourned to give people time to think further, research the subject, or consult colleagues.

3. *Subcommittee.* The subject can be referred to a subcommittee or working party, with instructions to report back to a later meeting.

4. *Vote.* A vote can be taken. This is usually by a simple show of hands, but important matters or those involving personalities may be put to a secret ballot. Sometimes a recorded vote may be requested, in which each individual's vote is entered in the record of the meeting.

It is not usual for the Chair to vote unless there is a tie, in which case he is normally regarded as having a casting vote.

Any other business

The Chair should not allow important issues to be raised at this stage, unless there is a genuine emergency which must be resolved before another meeting can be held.

Effective secretaryship

It is best if the Chair and Secretary are separate people as it is almost impossible for someone to be an efficient Chair while taking good notes and carrying out the other secretarial duties.

The Secretary should be chosen in advance of a meeting, as he has an important role during the preparation. Unskilled and unprepared office secretaries do not usually do a good job at meetings. The use of the word 'secretary' for employees who do typing and shorthand can cause confusion. They often lack the skills to be meeting secretaries, may not fully understand the points at issue, and may take extensive shorthand notes which take as long to work through as the original meeting.

Bright young junior staff – 'high fliers' – often make good meeting secretaries, and will also gain (one way or another) by exposure to the thinking of their elders and betters.

The duties of the Secretary include:

- administration and housekeeping
- supporting the Chair
- note-taking
- knowing the rules.

Administration and housekeeping

The Secretary should help the Chair to welcome other participants, and ensure that all administrative arrangements are complete. These include:

- freedom from interruption (phones and callers)
- room layout and equipment
- checking all visual aids
- room ventilation, heating, and freedom from visual and noise distractions
- refreshments
- loos and cloakrooms
- car parks
- message-taking arrangements.

Supporting the Chair

There is something about the ideal Secretary that is similar to the gentleman's gentleman. He does whatever is necessary to give his Chair practical and moral support, and this may involve helping him to:

- remember names (by judicious prompting, or perhaps by a diagram of the seating)
- keep time, especially for breaks and final conclusion
- remember promises (eg for participants to raise matters at a later stage)
- use correct procedures.

Note-taking

Notes and minutes are virtually the same; the records of more formal meetings are called 'minutes', those of less formal are usually called 'notes'. (Both will be called notes in the remainder of this section.)

Notes may be verbatim, a full discussion record, summary, or decision only in format.

Verbatim notes. These are used for Parliamentary and some court procedures, and are unlikely to concern us.

A full discussion record. This includes summaries of all the main contributions during a debate. It is appropriate for an academic colloquium, a political debate or negotiation. Notes of all the principal contributions will be needed.

Summary notes. These are the most common and most useful form of meeting notes. They do not record all, or even most, of what is said during a discussion. The exact degree of detail depends on the wishes of the Chair. Normally, the record should simply state the conclusions reached, possibly with a summary of the main reasons, and certainly with a list of actions to be taken and those responsible for them. The latter are often listed against each item in a separate column on the right of the paper. Occasionally, a participant may ask for his opinion to be recorded, and this should always be done. An example of summary notes is given on page 108.

Decision only record. This is used for most formal meetings.

Taking notes during a meeting needs practice. It is essential to note each speaker's name as soon as he starts. Most meeting secretaries use their own private shorthand, but it is a mistake to attempt a verbatim record when this will not be required. The art is to listen until a point has been made and understood, and then record it briefly.

Knowing the rules

In regular, more formal meetings of a company, club or society, the Secretary is the authority to whom all look for knowledge of the rules, articles of association, standing orders or bylaws by which proceedings are controlled. In less formal meetings, the Chair is more likely to be the authority, but the Secretary can often help in times of doubt.

Effective participation

As already noted, the responsibility for an ineffective meeting often lies with the participants. Before the meeting the most common fault is lack of preparation. At the meeting, the good participant makes the best contribution he can, while avoiding breaches of procedure or shows of temperament.

Making the best contribution

During preparation, participants will become clear as to what, if anything, they feel able to contribute to each item by way of knowledge or opinion. Many find it helpful to note such points down.

Hidden agendas

Many participants have political or personal objectives: what is often called the 'hidden agenda'. They may wish to lend support to a particular individual or faction, to impress their boss, or hide their own particular failings or lack of action.

It is unrealistic to pretend that such objectives do not exist, and obviously they are not wrong in themselves. However, the existence of such hidden agendas is one of the causes of ineffective meetings. A good leader will be sensitive to them, and good participants will be sensible in how far they allow them to affect their behaviour.

Timing

One of the hardest aspects of meeting participation is judging when to make a contribution.

If we come in at the start of a discussion, we can set the tone and help to control the way it develops.

It may be better to watch for another contribution that can act as a suitable trigger to our own. We can come in after a rather badly expressed or unpopular contribution on the opposite side of the question, thus capitalising on the meeting's badwill to the previous speaker, or we can look for an opportunity in a line of thought sympathetic to our own viewpoint which we can develop further. There may be obvious errors or gaps in what has so far been said.

Sometimes we will judge it best to hold back for as long as possible, until we have the feel of the meeting and other participants, or until others are exhausted or at a loss how to proceed.

Saying one's piece

The act of addressing a meeting makes use of the skills of speaking in public described in Chapter 4.

Faults of procedure

There are a few rules of procedure which apply in all meetings, however informal. These include obedience to the Chair, speaking only when invited by him, sticking to the subject, debating 'through the Chair', and interrupting only for procedural reasons.

Obedience to the Chair. This is a natural rule, without which anarchy would prevail. It sometimes helps to remember that we are obeying not the individual, but the office he holds; Chairs are, like the rest of us, fallible, but as long as they hold office, they are in charge.

There are two possible courses for an aggrieved participant. There may be a procedure available under which the Chair can be changed, provided a sufficient proportion of participants agree. However, this is a destructive process, and should only be used with the greatest care and circumspection. Failing this, the unhappy participant should make his point as simply and clearly as possible. In extreme cases, he may feel the only course is for him to leave the meeting.

Speaking only when invited by the Chair. At conferences and the most formal debates, it may be necessary to apply in writing to participate in a discussion.

In most meetings, there is an agreed method of attracting the attention of the Chair. In more formal meetings, the participant is called by name; in less formal, the Chair simply makes eye contact, or perhaps smiles or nods in his direction.

Sticking to the subject. This seems natural enough, but does not always happen. A participant may deliberately diverge, in order to waste time, or to make a point he has had no other opportunity of making. In such cases, the Chair is fully justified in calling him to order.

On the other hand, the participant may not be really clear what the subject is or what stage the debate has reached. This may be the fault of either party, but whoever is to blame it is the Chair's task to sort it out.

Debating 'through the Chair'. This is the convention by which participants speak not to one another, but address all they have to say to the Chair. It helps to smooth debate by taking some of the steam out of personal disagreements, it kicks the discussional football to the Chair, helping him to keep control and avoid a splintering of the meeting with several participants talking to each other.

Interrupting only for procedural reasons. Just as participants should only speak when asked by the Chair, so they should not normally interrupt others. It is a basic rule of democratic debate that all should have a hearing, however unpopular their opinion or their personality. A debate in which interruption is uncontrolled rapidly degenerates into chaos.

The rules of procedure for formal meetings are complex, and mostly inapplicable in day-to-day meetings. However, some are based on common sense and have value at any meeting. These include points of order, of explanation and of information.

To raise a *point of order* is to question whether the conduct of the meeting is correct. The decision on whether the point is justified will lie with the Chair, and having raised and tried to justify it, the participant must accept his ruling.

A *point of explanation* seeks to correct a misunderstanding about or misrepresentation of something we have said. It should be used sparingly, and only when there is a definite error.

A *point of information* seeks to help the meeting by providing facts that the current speaker does not know. Again, it should be used sparingly to provide only information that is both important and relevant.

Faults of temperament

Some of the worst problems in meetings arise because they expose individual character. Shyness, sensitivity, sulkiness, talkativeness, conceit and aggression become obvious to all. Interpersonal tensions also tend to surface to a degree which is not apparent in other contracts; if X hates Y's guts, the rest of the meeting will soon notice.

These problems provide another argument for a degree of formality: the more formal a meeting, the less effect they are likely to have on its proceedings.

Good follow-up

A meeting is not finished with when the participants leave. The record must be completed and circulated, and most important of all, agreed actions must be carried out. Only then will it have been worthwhile.

The record

The notes or minutes must be written up by the Secretary and approved by the Chair. The sooner this is done, the better. If they can be with participants the next day, this will demonstrate efficiency and allow the maximum time for any action to be completed. Memory will also still be fresh, gaps easier to fill and mistakes easier to rectify than at a later stage.

If the meeting was long or complex, or the issues unusually delicate, it may be worth producing draft minutes for circulation, at least to principal officials.

Whatever form is adopted, notes must be headed by the title, date and place of the meeting, followed by a list of those present, with the Chair at the top. In formal meetings, the list will be divided into those 'present' – the actual members of the meeting (usually elected, or by virtue of an office they hold), and those 'in attendance' – those who have a duty to serve the elected members (Secretary, Minutes Secretary etc).

The remainder of the notes should be split into numbered sections corresponding with the items on the agenda, each with its own heading.

Notes and minutes are always written as reported speech. This means:

- Using the past tense of verbs (eg 'The meeting agrees that . . .' becomes 'The meeting agreed that . . .').
- Changing 'I' to 'he', 'we' to 'they', 'us' to 'them', 'you' to 'he' or 'him' (if only one person) or 'they' or 'them' if more than one ('I told you we were wrong' becomes 'He told them they were wrong').
- Changing references to days and times as necessary ('today' becomes 'that day', 'now' becomes 'then', etc).

The notes may require circulating not only to those present, but also to others who have a need to know; they can form an effective method of communication within an organisation (provided there are not too many in circulation).

Agreed action

The meeting will only be justified when the agreed actions have been carried out and the agreed decisions implemented. The meeting that can report 100 per cent success in implementation can hold up its head in any company.

Summary notes

MEETING

of the

EXECUTIVE COMMITTEE OF THE HELLFIRE CLUB

on 29 February 1772

at

THE GOLDEN BALL, WEST WYCOMBE

PRESENT

Brother Black (Chair)
Brother Blue
Brother Brown
Brother Green
Brother Mauve
Brother Red
Brother Yellow (Treasurer)

IN ATTENDANCE
Brother Pink (Secretary)

1. APOLOGIES
Bros Purple, Violet and White.

2. MINUTES OF THE PREVIOUS MEETING
The Minutes of the meeting held on 25 December 1771 were read.

Bro Green stated that he had not suggested ordering an additional 30 cases of wine for Black Mass celebrations during January, as reported. The wine was needed for use by Brothers called on to visit the sick.

Bro Black pointed out that 'emanation' was wrongly spelt on page 3 line 4.

These amendments were accepted, and the Minutes were then signed.

---

3. MATTERS ARISING
The Chairman indicated that he had contacted the Grand Wizard of Worms, as requested, and was to meet him later that month. There were no other matters arising.

4. REPORT ON ORGY – 26 DECEMBER 1771
The Treasurer reported that the Orgy had made a loss of £13.40, largely due to the hire of costumes for Lady Companions and the overtime payments made to cleaning staff.

Attendance had been 34 Brothers, 12 Associate Brothers and 188 Lady Companions. There had been some complaint about the standard of refreshments, which had been taken up with the caterer. Otherwise, all present appeared to have had a wildly successful time.

The report was accepted.

5. HOME OF REST FOR DECREPIT BROTHERS
Bro Red presented a verbal report indicating that the cost of the project would now exceed the original budget, and that completion was unlikely before Halloween 1773.

There was considerable discussion, during which it was suggested that a working party should be formed to resolve difficulties with the sub-contractors. This was agreed, and Bros Blue, Green and Yellow were nominated and agreed to serve. The working party was instructed to report to the next meeting of the executive.

6. WITCHES' SABBATH
The Chairman said it had proved difficult to find a location with the requisite facilities. Grandwet Inns were unable to offer accommodation this year.

A number of suggestions were considered by the meeting, and it was felt that the best option might be a suitable blasted heath. Bro Mauve asked that his disagreement with this, on the grounds that it would be bad for Brothers with rheumatic complaints, should be minuted.

Bro Yellow was asked to investigate and report to the next meeting.
Action Bro Yellow

7. ANY OTHER BUSINESS
7.1 Bro Blue requested that smoking should be prohibited at future meetings of the executive. After discussion, this was not agreed.
7.2 Bro Green said that he had found a possible new supplier of insignia of higher quality at a lower price. He was asked to obtain quotations and report to the next meeting.
Action Bro Green

8. DATE OF NEXT MEETING
This was agreed for midnight on Candlemas in the Golden Ball.

(Reproduced from *How to Make Meetings Work*, Malcolm Peel, Kogan Page, 1988)

Meetings – the top 20

The top 10 dos
1. Do set clear objectives for every meeting.
2. Do circulate agenda and papers in advance.
3. Do complete thorough personal preparation.
4. Do choose a suitable room and lay it out carefully.
5. Do stick firmly to the agenda.
6. Do use visual aids as a help to control and discussion.
7. Do time your contributions carefully.
8. Do use the skills and knowledge of all participants.
9. Do restrain the verbose and self-opinionated.
10. Do use time sensibly throughout.

The top 10 don'ts
1. Don't hold a meeting, especially a 'regular' one, unless it is really necessary.
2. Don't invite people who do not need to attend.
3. Don't accept a meeting invitation unless you have a valid reason to attend.
4. Don't wait for latecomers unless there are special reasons to do so.
5. Don't let personal feelings affect meeting behaviour.
6. Don't mix creativity and criticism in the same phase of a discussion.
7. Don't allow or take part in more than one discussion at a time.
8. Don't attempt to force a decision before adequate debate.
9. Don't argue directly with other participants; debate through the Chair.
10. Don't, when in the Chair, express your own views unless it is essential to do so.

Chapter 6

The Media Face to Face

The word 'media' is commonly used to mean the main media of mass communication: radio, television, newspapers and magazines.

Most of the material used by the media is produced by professionals who work for a media organisation, but some is produced by freelances, who either make a living from this work or contribute occasionally.

The content – the stories – is often drawn from current events, and thus many other people are involved with the media. In some cases this involvement is sought; we can use the media for our own ends – to sell a product or service, raise awareness of what we do, improve our image, or persuade others of our beliefs. In other cases, media attention is thrust upon us, perhaps because we have featured in a court case, been involved in some newsworthy event or done something meritorious.

Large organisations usually employ the services of public relations professionals to smooth contacts with the media. Smaller organisations and individuals usually handle them direct. Even when public relations help is available, direct contact between protagonist and media is often necessary.

Contact between public and media includes:

- handling queries
- giving interviews
- press conferences and launches
- news releases
- advertising.

In this chapter, we will cover the first three; the last two are covered in Chapter 9.

Handling queries

Media communication is often two-way: we plan to use the media, and the media plan to use us. Ideally, the two intentions will match; news releases or articles will stimulate such interest that favourable editorial coverage or news items will be produced.

We may even find ourselves the subject of media reports unknowingly, although this is rare for those who are not public figures. In most cases, we will be approached by reporters or journalists who will question us by telephone, call on us (by appointment or without) or invite us to give interviews. If we are really famous (or notorious), they may shadow us or wait, disguised as bushes, at the bottom of the garden. However, unless we appear to offer a major story, most media queries are made by telephone.

Identification

It is important to learn as soon as possible who is quizzing us and why. In straightforward enquiries, journalists will always indicate this at the start of a conversation. If speaking over the phone, we must ensure that we give no information until we are satisfied who we are giving it to and for what purpose.

Very occasionally, deceit may be attempted, as when journalists gain entry to a hospital by claiming to be relatives of injured people, but this is rare in the business world.

Industrial espionage may occasionally be attempted by someone pretending to be a media representative, but this is probably even rarer.

Stick to the rules

Many organisations have rules about who may make statements to the media or answer their questions. For our own and our organisation's protection, we should know any such rules and stick to them.

A particularly important reason for such rules is that the media must get a consistent story. It must be impossible for reporters to get different answers to the same question by contacting two different people, and we must never fall into this trap.

Resist flattery

Most of us feel flattered and important when contacted and questioned by a media representative. While this is natural, it may make us flustered and less able to think straight.

Even worse, it may cause us to distort, by however little, our replies. It is hard to admit to the waiting world that we have nothing of interest to tell them, or that our achievements are of no significance. But if this is the truth, the only sensible course is to make it clear from the start. Otherwise, the feeling of importance may drag us step by step on to false ground, and we may end up as the hero of a news item which makes us the laughing-stock of everyone who knows us.

Check facts and admit ignorance

People are quick to blame the media for getting their facts wrong, but not so many are prepared to accept that they may have played a part in this process.

Checking facts involves additional work which journalists are usually reluctant to undertake. Moreover, if the numbers sound a little higher, or the facts a little more unusual than expected, the story will be that bit better.

It is always best to state only facts and figures of which we are certain and check that they have been heard and registered correctly. If we do not know, we should say so clearly; the media do not like uncertainty in a story, and a guess will always be turned into a firm statement.

Don't speak for too long

The feeling that the world is at last listening may tempt us to say too much. Apart from the boredom this is likely to cause, it can lead to indiscretion. Policemen and barristers know that the first rule of interrogation or cross-examination is to get the suspect or witness talking freely. What he says doesn't matter to start with; it's what he admits later that counts.

Don't give confidences

To attempt to speak to the media 'off the record' is in most situations a contradiction in terms. It puts an unfair pressure on the journalist, whose job is to get the best story he can. Some journalists may respect confidences, but others feel this is not part of their job. A wise person will not take the risk nor say anything he is not prepared to see staring at him in cold print the next day.

Be friendly

Most journalists respond to normal courtesy and friendliness. Although many are willing to accept an occasional drink, they will resist attempts to manipulate them.

Be available

Those who want good and extensive media coverage must be available both physically and politically.

Physically the media must know how to contact us, preferably 24 hours a day. At least one such name and telephone number should be in the possession of any media we believe could be interested in our activities.

Politically to be 'not available for comment' invariably puts the party so described in a weak and unfavourable light. Our comments must be planned and made by the right person, but for media success they must always be available.

Being interviewed

Radio and television interviews may be a very demanding experience for the unpractised, but if we want media exposure, it is one we must court. Although we are unlikely to face the TV cameras at peak viewing time, local radio interviews are available to anyone with a story, and if we really wish to use the media, we cannot shirk any opportunities.

Media interviews do not differ in kind from others, but there are a few additional points to bear in mind.

Before you accept

When inviting you to interview, the interviewer or someone from the production team should satisfy you as to what is intended. You will need to know:

- the subject of the interview
- what programme it is to be part of
- whether it is related to a news item
- whether anyone else is being interviewed about the same or related subjects
- whether it will be live or recorded
- who will conduct the interview
- the areas to be explored
- the time and place of the interview.

Location

Radio interviews may be held in a studio, a radio car, your office or home, or some relevant location. They can also be conducted by link-up on the public telephone network.

Interviewers prefer to use a studio, as this is less time-consuming for them, and the quality of sound is better. Although interviewees may believe a studio to be forbidding and prefer a more familiar location, they are unlikely to be given the choice. In fact, studios can be interesting places.

The second preference is usually a telephone interview. This can be carried out with the barest warning, although, unless we have really hot news, some notice is usually given.

Interviews conducted at our home, place of work or on location must normally be planned in advance. Home ground gives us the advantages of familiarity, easy access to documents and other requirements, and the initiative given by the role of host. However, such interviews are time-consuming for the interviewer, and if we really want to be interviewed we will be unwise to insist.

Preparation

It will help to listen to or watch a previous edition of the programme involved. This will tell us a great deal about the programme style and the interviewer's methods. Failing this, we should read the write-up in published programme listings such as the *Radio Times* or *TV Times*.

It is essential to have facts and figures at one's fingertips. In radio interviews we can refer to notes, but this is all but impossible in front of the TV camera.

Into the studio

If the interview is to be held in a studio, our first concern will be to get there. If it is going out live, it will, like time and tide, not wait for us. The only thing worse than arriving at the last moment, hot, flustered and tense, is not arriving at all.

Large studios have good reception arrangements and friendly receptionists who are used to handling interviewees of all types from the nervous to the self-important. Local radio stations may, particularly after hours, have nothing but an entryphone, which will not always be answered quickly or by someone who is expecting us.

Radio tapes

If the interview is being taped for radio, we are likely to be conducted into a small, dark, untidy cubby-hole. Somewhere in the gloom will be a fabric-covered table, above which will be the one essential; the microphone. We should sit as comfortably as we can within a couple of feet or so of the mike, and arrange essential papers (of which there should be very few) on the table so that we can see them without turning away or moving them noisily.

The interviewer will check for sound levels, while getting a conversation going and helping us to relax. He will probably outline one or two of the principal questions he intends to ask us. He will then set the tape going. Some interviewees talk as in a normal conversation, looking at the interviewer and reacting to his facial expression and body language.

Others concentrate solely on the voice and avoid the distraction of sight, even shutting their eyes. Either method can work; the choice is ours.

Listen with care. It is essential to listen to questions with care. Experienced media interviewers do not aim to catch the interviewee out. Rather, they ask a question and then enlarge on it, thus allowing us to collect our thoughts while they talk. We should pick up this rhythm and make use of the thinking time it gives. For example, the leader of an action group calling for a new road to be built might be asked:

> *'Surely there are many people who object strongly to the proposed road? Although your group wants it, a lot of residents claim it would damage their property, add to pollution and destroy a particularly beautiful stretch of countryside. How do you answer them?'*

The ideal answer. As the voice is the only means of communication, we must take particular care to project well. It is best to use a normal speaking voice; indeed, the best broadcasters speak as they would to a friend sitting next to them. However, words should be spoken clearly and unhurriedly, in a lower rather than a higher pitch.

We must convey interest and conviction in all our replies, avoiding tones or hesitations that might be interpreted as doubt or uncertainty. It is better to give a partially correct reply with conviction than an entirely accurate reply with faltering and hesitancy.

We should avoid leading up to an answer gradually, as this can sound evasive and lose the listeners' attention. If the interview is being taped, there is also a danger that our key point may be edited out; like journal editors, tape editors tend to cut from the bottom. If the interview is live, time pressure may prevent us ever reaching a major point that we have kept back too long. At worst, we may lose our own way.

For example, an inexperienced interviewee might try to reply to the question above by saying:

> *'Yes, there is bound to be opposition to a big scheme like this. We have held 15 meetings now and been round door to door, and we have had a really encouraging response almost everywhere except on Gypsy Lane. There is very little property that would be damaged; only three houses, or four at most, would have to go, and the owners would be fully compensated of course. In any case, we know the majority are in favour . . .'*

A good answer starts promptly with a clear, bright statement, followed by a few sentences of explanation. We need not stick too closely to the exact words used by the interviewer, but should reply to the spirit of the question.

For example, a better reply to the same question would be:

'We understand their feelings. However, it simply isn't possible to please everyone in a big scheme like this and the plan we are putting forward is the best compromise. We do know what people are thinking – we have talked face to face with as many as we can. When they understand our proposal fully most people see the great benefits it offers the community as a whole.'

It is best to reply immediately, like an actor coming in on cue; if we need to hesitate, we can do it more convincingly after we have started.

Too many facts and figures become confusing and counter-productive; we should ration ourself to those that are both immediately telling and supportive of our case.

Action replays. Interviewers sometimes offer and always give on request the opportunity to rehear some or all of an interview, followed by a second attempt at a passage either party is unhappy with. It is not a good idea to fiddle around with an interview too much; answers often get worse rather than better, and will certainly lack spontaneity and life. Taped interviews are, in any case, virtually always edited down, often to a small fraction of the original length.

Live radio

For a live radio interview or discussion, we are shown into a room containing a console and other gadgetry separated by a glass screen from the studio. If we are lucky, we may have the chance to meet our interviewer before the programme, but often he is already on air.

At a suitable moment, we are shown into the studio and motioned to sit near the interviewer and a mike. Music is often being transmitted at this point, and if the studio mikes are dead, the interviewer welcomes us and perhaps gives an indication of the questions he intends to ask. The moment when we go on air is usually indicated by a red light, and certainly by the motions of the interviewer.

From this point, the process is identical to the taped interview, except that (*a*) there is only one chance, and (*b*) we may be put under time pressure. We should always avoid going on too long with any answer; both interviewers and listeners become nervous if an interviewee appears to suffer from verbal diarrhoea.

Interviewers usually indicate the time available by the form of their question. For example:

'Now, finally, Mr Green, what is your answer to people who say . . .?'

'Very briefly, what do you see as the next step?'

We must be sure to pick up such hints, or we risk interruption in full flow and will lose the chance of a crisp, authoritative conclusion.

Many people find live interviews set the adrenalin flowing, and are stimulated to giving a more sparkling performance than they would achieve in front of a tape recorder. Live interviews can be great fun, and become addictive.

Telephone interviews and link-ups

If the interview is being conducted at a distance, this may be done by telephone, or by land-line from a local studio. Sound quality is at its worst over the phone, hence we are more likely to be invited to the nearest studio. Once there, we are given headphones through which we can hear what is going on at the other end. We do not have the option of interpreting the body language of the interviewer, and will have to concentrate purely on sound.

TV interviews

The most powerful weapon of mass communication we are ever likely to wield is an appearance on television. By the same token, we must get such an interview right.

Appearance. The first difference from radio is the need to consider appearance. We must be neither over- nor under-dressed; our clothes must be appropriate for the occasion and the image we wish to project. The colours should be tasteful and well-matched. White should be eschewed: it shows up blue in colour. Details such as ties, brooches or badges are important and will need particular thought. Our hair (if we have any) must be as we wish it to appear.

On arrival at the studio, we shall quickly be made aware of the need for make-up. This is to allow for the intense lighting and for the heat it generates. Men may find this off-putting, but the professionals who apply make-up are skilled, understanding and use it as sparingly as practicable.

The studio itself is likely to be immense, one-half brightly lit and nearly empty, the other in darkness and swarming with people. The interview takes place in the lit section. Unless it is a solo performance at the end of a land-line, the layout of furniture is unlikely to allow us the use of crib sheets or other paperwork.

It is helpful to know which camera is transmitting at any given moment, and this is indicated by a red light. It is not usually effective to talk to camera; we should ignore them and use normal eye contact with the interviewer or others in the group. We must remember that the cameras may picture us not only when we are talking, but when we are listening; we are 'on stage' the whole time.

Interviewing style. TV favours a relaxed, intimate style, and we should cultivate a warm, friendly smile even under pressure. We must avoid too much movement of body or head, and signs of tension such as clenched hands or fiddling with pencils.

The questioning techniques employed are much the same as for radio, except in the case of distinguished and controversial public figures who might rate a hostile approach. It does not make good viewing to reduce an interviewee to nonsense, so we are likely to get a chance to state our case. However, time is severely limited, and it is essential to get our principal point in at the earliest opportunity, or we may never reach it.

The suggestions made in discussing radio interviews, particularly 'The ideal answer' (page 116), are applicable to TV interviews.

Background. Television interviews outside the studio raise the question 'What does the viewer see apart from the talking heads?' We should try to control this, considering what image of ourselves and our circumstances the background will convey.

Background can indicate that we are well off or poor; that we have luxurious or popular taste. It can suggest scholarship (by rows of books), tidiness or untidiness, a hi-tech environment or relaxed domesticity. An office can suggest pompous authority or businesslike efficiency.

We must resist the temptation to show off home, office or possessions; viewers spot such vanity at once. Rather, we must use the background to reinforce the message we wish to convey; viewers are likely to see and remember at least as much of it as of anything we say.

Press conferences and launches

What are our objectives?
To be successful, we must have clear objectives for holding a press conference.

To say that our objectives are to get media coverage is not sufficient. We can achieve this by means of a good news release without exposing ourselves to the risks or incurring a fraction of the cost of a press conference.

The kinds of event that the media regard as justifying a conference include hot news, a contribution to a major controversy, the presence of an important person, or the launch of something – whether a book, an election campaign, a product or a ship.

None of these will make a successful conference without the presence of at least one principal and knowledgeable person who can be questioned in depth about the subject. The author, the candidate, the victim, the inventor or whoever *must* be available; a press conference is no place for substitutes.

Time and place

We must choose a time and place that are convenient for as many as possible of the reporters we want. However, the choice of timing is always partly in the lap of the gods; if another event of apparently greater interest intervenes, our conference will sink without trace.

We must also find out whether anyone else is planning a competing event. If so, we can try to upstage them by holding ours first, or even, if we are certain of the strength of our position, at the same time. In some situations, a better strategy may be to fit in with the plans of our rivals – as with the election press conferences of different parties.

The location should either be very convenient or very attractive. Aiming at convenience, we will probably choose an urban hotel. Our offices or those of our PR agent will do only if they are central, well served by public transport and have the necessary facilities. Aiming at attractiveness may prove expensive, as it could involve chartering Concorde, the Orient Express or someone's yacht.

Often, a more appropriate location might be the scene of the crime, the doctor's laboratory, or gathered round the Thing Itself (whatever the Thing is). This offers special local colour, the chance to meet everyone involved and good photo opportunities. However, if it is off the beaten track it increases the risk of low attendance.

Preparation

Generally speaking, the less interesting the subject the more expensive and detailed the preparation needs to be; hot news requires little more than space for a meeting and some quick phone calls. The press will flock to see the only bottle of the unique, instant cure-all we have at last produced and proved, especially if those who owe their lives to it are also present. On the other hand, the conference for the launch of our 1990 catalogue may succeed only in a high-class hotel with a good deal of smoked salmon, alcohol and nice personal invitations sent out weeks in advance.

The plan. Press conferences and launches can be planned in almost any way, but they must be planned, for chaos is always waiting round the corner.

The simplest plan is: reception; presentation; questions; informal discussion. The reception period allows the media time to assemble, pick up news releases or information packs, and meet representatives of the organisation informally. The presentation reinforces the material in the release and exposes the individual(s) most involved. The question and answer session is at the heart of a successful event, and calls for careful anticipation. The final informal discussion, often during appropriate hospitality, provides an opportunity to exchange additional information and forge real relationships.

Briefing. To make a successful press conference, the person most involved in the subject must be exposed. The candidate may have his agent, the chairman his public affairs director, the author his publisher, but the smaller the part these advisers play, the better.

It is essential, therefore, that the principal is thoroughly briefed. He has put himself on show, and must have what it takes. If he is familiar with Chapter 4, especially 'Dealing with questions' (page 85), he will be well placed. The sections of this chapter on radio interviews, especially 'The ideal answer' (page 116), will also prove useful.

It should go without saying that the advisers and supporters must also be well briefed, even though their knowledge may be used mainly in one-to-one conversation over the buffet. It is important that conflicting answers are not given, and it can sometimes be wise to decide in advance who, and who alone, will answer on particular aspects.

All briefings should include advice on who is likely to be present, from which media, and anything known about their editor.

The news release. Although the essence of the conference is the questions and answers, a news release, embargoed until after the conference has finished, should be given to all present. Chapter 9 makes suggestions for writing good releases.

For more complex conferences and launches, we need to prepare information packs contained in folders which include general information about our organisation, copies of any reports or documentation to be discussed, and biographies of the leading personalities, as well as the news release itself.

Invitations
We should develop and cultivate our own list of press contacts.

Media relationships. A genuine relationship with an editor, correspondent, producer or reporter is far more likely to bring an acceptance than 20 scattered invitations.

The idea that media people are to be wooed with alcohol and trips on Concorde has become something of a travesty. Those who wish to make good long-term use of the media will cultivate such relationships on a basis of mutual respect and friendship. The most worthwhile coverage, certainly over the long term, comes from knowing the interests of journals and journalists, and showing that we know and can meet those interests. Occasional meetings for a relaxed chat, even though we have little to report; providing tips about news we have heard, even though it is not ours; giving the best chance of using anything big we may have; invariably playing straight in terms of equal opportunities; these are ingredients in successful cultivation of the media.

The general list. In addition to our close contacts we shall want to invite others to obtain the widest coverage. We should use a listing such as *Willings Press Guide* to ensure that we cover all suitable local papers, local radio and TV stations, and the appropriate trade press.

We shall also hope for the national media, but in the absence of real news interest, personal relationship, or the most extravagant of locations (something that could easily lead to unfavourable editorial comment), this will usually remain a hope only.

If we do not know a named individual to invite and have doubts as to who might be most interested, it is best to address the invitation to 'The Editor'.

Conduct of the conference

Press conferences have no rules, and their conduct depends on the nature of the occasion, the numbers present, the location and the extent of the hospitality. To work properly they require direction and control, and the various elements call for most of the communication skills discussed elsewhere in this book.

Face-to-face skills are needed in the contacts between the individual representatives of the organisation and the media with which most conferences begin and end. Chairing and other meeting skills will be required in running the main presentations and the following question and answer session. Oral presentation skills are required for the main session. Skilful writing is needed in preparing the news release.

The media face to face – the top 20

The top 10 dos
1. Do check who is asking questions and why.
2. Do know the organisation's rules about media contacts.
3. Do stick to facts and admit ignorance.
4. Do consider clothes, turnout and background for TV interviews.
5. Do arrive in good time for radio and TV interviews.
6. Do listen carefully to questions.
7. Do adopt a relaxed and friendly but alert style.
8. Do reply crisply, making the main point at the start and elaborating, if necessary, afterwards.
9. Do plan press conferences carefully.
10. Do cultivate good long-term media relationships.

The top 10 don'ts
1. Don't give confidences or make off-the-record comments.
2. Don't be 'unavailable for comment'.
3. Don't exaggerate, especially about one's own involvement or achievements.
4. Don't sound hesitant or uncertain in replies.
5. Don't quote too many facts or figures.
6. Don't go on too long with a reply.
7. Don't talk to the camera during a TV interview (unless it is being conducted from a remote location).
8. Don't call a press conference if a news release will do as well.
9. Don't try to manipulate media representatives.
10. Don't attack others publicly without the most thorough thought and preparation.

Part 2

Written Communication

Chapter 7

Letters, Memos and Other Office Communications

Letters are produced to be sent outside an organisation, but memos (short for 'memoranda') are written for internal use, and filenotes are memos written to preserve a record on our own papers. Newsletters and staff magazines are also used for internal communication, and share many features with letters and memos.

As communication technology has developed and travel become easier, the proportion of business transacted by letter has diminished, while the use of the telephone, face-to-face meetings and direct computer links has steadily increased. The only form of letter writing that has increased has been the production of the circular, or 'junk mail'.

However, the growth of facsimile transmission and the electronic mailbox has given letters and memos a new lease of life, and they should continue to play an important role for many years to come.

Letter writing

Letters are an efficient means of communication when:

- an agreement is being made or confirmed
- we need a record that we have communicated, or tried to
- the subject is complex or involves important facts or figures
- there are shades of meaning best conveyed in writing
- it is difficult to contact someone in other ways
- we need to give the same message to people in different locations.

Writing good letters is made easier by following a simple series of steps. These include:

- (if we are replying to a letter) read that letter with care
- clarify our message

- write the first draft
- revise the draft
- check the redraft
- produce the final letter.

} These steps are dispensed with when simple letters are written.

Read with care

One of the most common mistakes in letter writing is not to reply properly. The impression can be given that the letter has not been grasped, read, or even received. Questions may be answered wrongly, only in part, or not at all; points may be ignored or misunderstood. If the letter we are replying to is long, complicated or surprising, we should read it several times.

As a general rule, we should reply to a letter the day it is received. Sometimes the most sensible course is to pick up the telephone and clarify our doubts with the sender. If we are annoyed, we should put it away for a while (hours, even days) to give ourselves time to simmer down, or show it to others for interpretation, comment or advice.

For example, in trying to negotiate a business agreement, we might receive a letter such as:

Dear Fred

John and I have discussed our meeting with you yesterday, and your proposal to us.

Unfortunately, we decided that we could not accept it.

We didn't go along with you when you said you must have 'first refusal' of all work that resulted from our campaign; we think it would depend on where the work came from. Did you really mean that we would have to agree to buy up any goods unsold after six months? We don't quarrel with the prices, although we think there should be special prices for quantities over 100, and that it would be right to charge for delivery.

John and I are in touch with a couple of other people. If you would like to think further about these points, by all means come back to me, but we want to get things sorted out by the end of the month.

Yours,

Martin

Our reaction to this might be:

'I didn't say any of those things.'

'I feel mad; Martin is really trying to wind me up.'

'I still want to do business with the guy; he's the best contact I have.'

'Perhaps I should fix another meeting to sort things out; but then again it might make things worse. If I put my proposal on paper there's less chance he will misunderstand it.'

'Actually, he's really just trying to set up a bargaining position. I must keep my nerve and go on step by step.'

Clarify the message

If the letter we wish to write is straightforward, we can move immediately to the next step, and write the first draft (see below). If our letter seems likely to be complex, difficult or lengthy, we must first ensure that we have clarified the message we wish to convey.

To do this we should jot down notes in quick, headline form; we are not starting to write the letter, but organising our thoughts.

The 'message' will involve not only facts or figures, but also the attitude and reaction we want the recipient to know about. There may be social conventions or sensitive aspects to bear in mind, as in letters of condolence, when rejecting a job applicant or chasing a debt. In every case we must define what we wish to say and what to avoid saying.

In replying to the letter, we might note down such things as:

— *I want to reach an agreement, but not to give too much away. They are important to my chance of success, but not irreplaceable.*
— *I can agree about a price for more than 100, and also about charging for delivery.*
— *I think they know perfectly well I didn't say they would have to buy up unsold goods after six months, but I must keep cool.*
— *I want to maintain the bit about 'first refusal'. It would be essential, and in any case I don't think any other way would work.*

We would also decide the best order for our main points at this stage, writing a number against each item on the list.

Write the first draft

It is best to get the pen (or keyboard fingers) moving as quickly as possible. When writing a difficult letter, most people find it is better to get started and keep the ideas and words flowing rather than try to get it right first time. Editing and polishing can be done later.

If a word processor is being used, this approach is even more sensible, as alterations will be simpler to make.

Many people find it helps to write more than they will need in the final letter. It is easier to cut words out than to add them. For example, our first draft reply to the letter could be:

Dear Martin

Thanks for your letter. I don't really agree with a lot of what you say.

The idea about charging for delivery is OK, so we can agree there, provided you aren't going to suggest too much. £1 a mile up to 25 and then 50p a mile is what I would say.

As to a price for orders of more than 100, we could make it something like £195 a unit (provided they are for delivery at the same time, of course). We could think about larger orders, and perhaps regular ones, on a contract basis.

This all doesn't matter unless we can sort out the other things you accuse me of. I did not say anything about your buying up unsold units; this would be silly. Production is my business, and if I make too many, that's my funeral. In any case, I shall only be making to order, at least to start with.

I certainly did say that I wanted first refusal of any business you are offered during the sales campaign. That's only natural. For one thing it wouldn't be possible to be sure where the business came from. People often don't use our order forms, and lots telephone these days anyway. And often the person ordering isn't the person who saw that ad and made the decision to buy.

No, this must be make or break for me. The whole idea of the campaign is so we both win out, but if you passed orders to anyone else without giving me first chance, there's no way we could work together. This would have to be spelt right out.

There it is. If you want to talk it over again, give me a ring. Please let me know one way or the other quickly if you're not interested; I have other irons in the fire.

Dictating

If we have a secretary who likes using shorthand, or a dictating machine, we can dictate our letters.

Dictating is a skill in its own right but has its own problems. It is easy to lose the place or the thread of our thoughts, especially if we are interrupted. Some people find that dictating letters helps them to achieve a more relaxed, friendly style, but others find the reverse: when they dictate a letter it sounds pompous and stilted.

Dictating other than by machine also takes a great deal of secretarial time. As well as typing the letter, the secretary has to sit while we dictate it and cope with the inevitable interruptions. Dictating to a secretary makes some people feel important, but rarely helps overall efficiency.

Some organisations have centralised typing facilities in a pool of audio typists. Letters are transmitted to the pool by the internal telephone network or cassettes. Dictating for an audio typist requires full identification and instruction to be given at the start, and that all punctuation and special layout instructions should be given clearly at the appropriate point. For example:

> *'This is Fred White of Purchasing, extension 274. I am writing an ordinary company letterhead to go out today, first class, please. The letter is to James Kirkby Esq., Managing Director, Ectoplasm UK plc, 15 Ether Place, Glasgow, G3 6XJ. Dear James, Thank you for your letter of 23 July 1990, stop, paragraph. Since you wrote, comma, I have received a reply from Spirits Inc, stop. They say, colon, line space, indent paragraph, quotes: Unfortunately, comma, it is no longer possible to obtain supplies of the necessary raw materials, comma, and we therefore very much regret we are unable to meet your esteemed instructions, stop, close quotes, line space, margin. In the circumstances, comma, I cannot suggest any alternative, stop. Yours sincerely, Fred White, Executive, comma, Purchasing. Thank you.'*

Revise the draft

If the letter is straightforward, revision may not be necessary. If we have any doubts, we must revise.

We should let the draft lie for as long as possible before revision. An hour or two may be all we can spare, though particularly important or difficult letters can benefit from being slept on or even put on one side for a few days. This helps us to cool down, see things in a different perspective and perhaps generate new ideas.

If a letter has really annoyed us, and we have written a stinker of a reply, it can even be best to tear the draft up and start with a clean sheet. Writing it will at least have helped to relieve our feelings.

While revising, we should try to put ourselves in the position of the reader. The most helpful question is *not* 'What do I want to write?' but 'What do I want him to read?'

We should consider the following actions:

Choose the most appropriate style

Letters can be formal, semi-formal or friendly, but there has been a tendency for many years towards less formal styles.

The formal style is not often needed, but is appropriate when replying to formal invitations, writing to important people we do not know personally or perhaps in legal correspondence. The semi-formal style is most frequently used and is right for the wide range of business letters. We naturally choose the friendly approach when writing to those we know well.

Rearrange the order

To rearrange the order of paragraphs, sentences or phrases can often help to make the flow smoother and more logical. With a word processor, making such changes is easy.

Cut out

Provided it says all that needs saying, the shorter a letter is, the better. Padding is always wrong. Repetition often creeps in. We should ruthlessly axe anything that does not add to the message.

Some words, such as 'very', 'actually', 'quite', 'fully', 'naturally', 'certain', 'rather', 'simply' and 'perhaps' add little. Adverbs are always strong candidates for the red pencil.

Most writers are addicted to certain words: 'particular', 'important', 'significant' and 'undoubted' are common culprits. Addictive phrases include: 'at the end of the day', 'all too easily', 'in point of fact', 'on the other hand'. Even everyday phrases such as 'there is . . .' or 'there are . . .' are often superfluous. We must spot our own weaknesses and eradicate them.

Choose words with care

Nothing is gained by using long or impressive sounding words just for the sake of it.

The two main sources of English words are Anglo-Saxon and Latin. Anglo-Saxon words are short (often of four letters) and say what they mean simply and directly. Latin words tend to be longer and sound more important. Here are one or two examples:

Anglo Saxon	Latin
gift	donation
buy	purchase
think	consider
last	ultimate
end	conclusion

In some cases, the Latin words add extra shades of meaning. If this is what we intend, we are right to use them, but we should be clear what this extra meaning is, and never choose words merely to impress.

We must also strive for accuracy. It is particularly dangerous to use any word unless we are sure of its meaning. A dictionary and a thesaurus (such as the *New Collins Thesaurus*) which lists words with similar meaning, are a great help.

Avoid jargon and unfamiliar abbreviations
A common mistake is to use words, phrases or abbreviations that are unknown to the addressee. If we use them regularly ourselves it is easy to fall into the trap of assuming that others are also familiar with them. We should challenge every abbreviation and technical or jargon term we have used, asking 'Am I sure the reader will understand this?'

Tone down
Toning down or cutting out strong expressions will avoid upsetting the addressee unintentionally or needlessly. What sounds like justifiable firmness when we write it can look like gratuitous rudeness when it arrives on someone else's desk.

Explain and give examples
We may be so clear in our own mind that we do not realise that others may not be: our more difficult points may benefit from explanation. Examples can be an even greater help; a good 'for instance' can sometimes do more than paragraphs of explanation.

Correct the grammar
Grammar and correct usage may frighten us, but need not. If we have doubts, the best strategy is to use short, simple sentences. These also make reading easier. There are several guides that can help, including the classic *Modern English Usage* by Fowler.

Check punctuation
Punctuation is made easier if we keep our sentences short and use more full stops than anything else. We should use commas sparingly, and avoid colons and semi-colons if we have the slightest doubt about their function.

Quotation marks should be used only to surround the exact words used by someone else, or a word we are about to define – *not* for reported speech or words about which we are self-conscious or uncertain. For example:

> *My director has told me that 'our report is one of the best he has read and he wants to implement it quickly'* is incorrect. If we wish to write this sentence, no quotation marks must be used.

> *My director told me 'Your report is one of the best I have read and I want to*

implement it quickly' is correct as we are quoting the exact words used.

I think our report is 'smashing' is incorrect. We should choose a word we are more confident about (eg excellent), or use the word we have chosen without the quotation marks.

Layout

Good layout can do a lot to improve the appearance and readability of a letter. If we have a secretary or typist, we will rely on him for good layout, but the responsibility always lies with the person who signs the letter.

We should use a fresh paragraph whenever we change the subject; long paragraphs put the reader off. It often makes the meaning clearer to list items, using numbers or 'bullets'. Quotations should be indented.

The result

After editing our draft letter (page 130), the result might be:

Dear Martin

Thanks for your letter. There is obviously a lot we agree about, and I am sure we can work together. There are just a couple of points we must resolve.

I agree that we should charge for delivery. A rate of £1 a mile up to 25 miles, and 50p a mile above that distance seems right.

I also agree the need for price breaks for large orders. We could go beyond 100. May I suggest:

  100–499:   £195 per unit
  500+:   £175 per unit

We could negotiate for larger or regular orders.

There has been a misunderstanding about buying up unsold units. I didn't say this; I shall only be making to order anyway.

I did say that I wanted first refusal of any business you were offered during our sales campaign. This seems to me the only practicable way. It would be impossible to know where orders came from. These days many are telephoned, and people don't always use our form when ordering by post. Often the person who orders didn't make the buying decision, and can't say where it came from. I am sure you will see it this way on reflection.

If there is anything you would like to talk over further, please give me a ring. I look forward to your reply.

Check the redraft

Important letters may need several redrafts; it is worth making the effort to ensure a good result.

If there is anyone else we can bring in at this stage to comment and advise, so much the better; a fresh mind brings a fresh approach, and may spot points of difficulty or offer ideas we had missed. A secretary will help with spelling, punctuation and grammar, and a word processor with a spelling check is a useful tool. However, the responsibility for a letter lies with the person who signs it, and this final check is our last chance to get it right.

The details to check include:

- greeting
- spelling
- conclusion
- signature
- copies
- enclosures.

Greeting

Most letters are now addressed: Dear Mr/Mrs/Ms (surname). Problems only arise if we do not know the name of the person we are writing to. We can put 'Dear Sir' with its sexist overtones, or 'Dear Sir or Madam'. However, both these convey a formal, cold feeling. We may feel we have to use them when writing a circular letter, although there are alternatives such as 'Dear Colleague', 'Dear Customer', 'Dear Fellow Director (or whatever)', etc.

If we know the recipient well, the letter will begin 'Dear (first name)'. Occasionally, we will have a problem judging whether we really do know the person well enough, especially if it is a female who has signed herself simply by her first and surnames. In this case it is probably wiser to reply: 'Dear Ms (surname)'.

Conclusion

If we have greeted the recipient as 'Dear Sir' or 'Dear Sir or Madam', the conventional ending is 'Yours faithfully'. An old-fashioned conclusion still occasionally used by those writing to up-market national papers is 'Yours etc'. In other cases, the universal practice is now to end 'Yours sincerely'.

If we know the recipient well, we can add 'Kind regards', 'Best wishes' or some similar phrase either before, instead of, or as well as 'Yours sincerely'. Around Christmas, it could be 'With the season's greetings' or 'With best wishes for Christmas and the New Year'.

Signature

The growing practice is to sign all letters with both first and surname. However, if we are writing in the formal style, initials and surname are more appropriate. When writing to a friend, it is usual to sign with our first (or perhaps nick-) name only.

On business correspondence the signature should be followed by the name typed or printed. Women may wish to add 'Mrs', 'Miss' or 'Ms'. This is less common than it was, but it does remove the doubt mentioned earlier as to how they prefer to be greeted in reply.

It is *not* usual for the name to be followed by degrees, decorations etc unless there is a special reason. A formal professional opinion, when the qualifications which entitle us to express such an opinion must be on the record, might provide such a reason.

In business letters, it is helpful to follow the typed name with the job title of the writer: partner, purchasing manager etc. Some top people in an organisation (such as chairman or chief executive) prefer not to do this, but this is only sensible if the heading of the paper carries their title.

Copies

If we are sending copies of a letter to someone other than the addressee, it is usual to add a note after the signature block: 'Copy to: W. Bloggs, Chief Accountant'. An alternative is to state this at a suitable point in the letter itself:

> *I imagine our chief accountant, Mr W Bloggs, will wish to reply to you on this point, and I am sending him a copy of this letter.*

If the copy or copies do not call for any specific action by the recipients, we can indicate this by writing 'For information'. This is frequently abbreviated as 'cfi'=copy for information. While there is no advantage in multiplying paper for the sake of it, an additional copy or two can aid communication and keep everyone who needs to know in the picture.

Occasionally, we will want to send a copy, perhaps to a colleague (eg to our boss, to show him how we are handling a particular problem), without drawing the attention of the addressee to the fact. In this case, the top copy will carry no note, but the copies will be endorsed 'Hidden (or 'Blind') copy; A Smith'.

We will, of course, always keep a copy for our files. Many people keep two copies of their business letters, one for the subject file and one on a day file kept in date order.

Enclosures

If we are enclosing anything with the letter, it is wise to say so, so that the addressee can check he has received everything safely, and also so that it is on record. This is usually stated after the signature block: 'Enc' is a standard abbreviation, although if there is more than one enclosure, or we want a more precise record, we may prefer to write more explicitly: 'Enclosed: copy of contract' etc.

Produce the final letter

We must not spoil the ship for a ha'porth of tar. Everything we have worked for must be there, 100 per cent correct, in the final product.

The paper must be the right size and quality. The writing or typing should be neat and clear, and preferably on one side of the page only – the result always looks neater and is easier to read, especially when filed.

The envelope must be of the right size; too small an envelope means the sheets have to be folded too many times, and may be damaged when being removed. Apart from the appearance of untidiness, many people are reluctant to read a letter that has been folded more than once; the more folds, the greater the reluctance. If it is a letter we were not expecting or do not want, this may even be enough to prevent us from reading it.

Letters are best folded with the writing outside. If more than one fold is unavoidable, it is better to fold across the sheet rather than from top to bottom. It is also best to fold so that the start is visible as soon as the letter is taken from its envelope.

Memos and filenotes

A memo (memorandum) is a letter sent to someone within the same organisation as the writer. A filenote is a memo written to place information on the record usually, as the name implies, on a file of correspondence and other papers.

Memos and filenotes should be written as carefully as letters. We may feel that a document that is not expected to be seen by outsiders does not require as much care, but this is a trap. There is as much scope for misunderstanding and as much danger of unfortunate consequences from a sloppily written memo or filenote as from a letter.

Because what we write is on the record, it is also impossible to be sure that it never will be seen outside the organisation. Many employees have lived to rue the day they wrote an incautious memo that subsequently found its way into the hands of a dissatisfied customer, the press or a court of law.

Memos and filenotes thus require the same approach as letters. However, there are differences in style, content and format:

Style

We are likely to know the addressee (or addressees, for memos are often copied to several people) well, and this must affect the style in which we write. We can usually come to the points we wish to make more directly, and will be able to assume more detailed knowledge of the subject and background. While we must avoid discourtesy (the word 'please' should often occur in memos), we shall rarely need to use circumlocutions or lengthy explanations solely out of politeness.

Content

There will be less need to avoid jargon and abbreviations. While we must never automatically assume that a reader within the same organisation knows what is meant, he is more likely to do so than if he were an outsider. Indeed, it may appear patronising and discourteous if we do not employ jargon and abbreviations which are in common use.

However, the dangers of ambiguity, vagueness or other sources of misunderstanding are as great as in any other written communication. In particular, we may mistakenly assume that what we understand is also understood in the same way by the addressee. If we have any doubt we should give a full, clear explanation.

Format

Many organisations have a standard format for memos. If such a guide is not available, we must give date, addresses, sender, copies to and the heading. The addressee and sender may be indicated by name, job title, location or initials only, depending on the organisational practice. The method of indicating copies and enclosures is the same as for letters.

An example, based on the letter used in the first part of this chapter, is shown opposite:

Newsletters

Newsletters are frequently used as a means of communication with members of a club or other organisations, especially if there are few occasions on which they can all meet together. Staff newsletters and magazines perform the same task in business organisations, and may also be used to communicate management policy and the achievements of the organisation.

In large organisations, staff magazines are often produced by an

To: *T Brown*   From: *J White*
    Contracts   *Marketing*

    c: P Green, Sales (Northern)
    M Black, Transport

                                     25 June 1990

SMITHS SALES CAMPAIGN

1. *I agree that we should charge for delivery. I suggest a rate of £1 a mile up to 25 miles, and 50p a mile above that distance.*

2. *I agree the price breaks for large orders. We could go beyond 100. I suggest:*
                       100–499: £195 per unit
                       500+:   £175 per unit
   Larger or regular orders should be subject to negotiation.

3. *We would have no obligation to buy up unsold units; the subcontractor will only make to order.*

4. *We must insist on first refusal of any business arising during the sales campaign. The sourcing of orders is impracticable because:*
   1. *Many are now telephoned*
   2. *Written orders may not be on our form*
   3. *The order-placer may not be the decision-taker, and often does not know how the choice was made.*

   Please confirm that I may go forward in these terms.

editorial department with extensive facilities similar to those of a newspaper or journal.

Club newsletters and those of smaller organisations often adopt the format of an open letter to members from an individual such as the chairman, managing director or the editor of the newsletter.

For success, such letters must:

- be topical and up to date
- use human interest stories as much as possible
- have many brief items rather than a few long ones
- be reader- rather than writer-oriented
- be as excitingly laid out as facilities allow, using pictures, cartoons, boxes and headlines. The advent of desk-top publishing makes such layouts much more practicable than hitherto.

The process of producing a newsletter follows the same steps as other letters (see earlier).

Letters and memos – the top 20

The top 10 dos
1. Do read the letter you are answering with care.
2. Do write a first draft quickly.
3. Do, when answering a letter, reply fully to all points.
4. Do let the first draft of a difficult letter lie for as long as practicable.
5. Do revise and edit the first draft ruthlessly.
6. Do put points in the best order for the reader.
7. Do use simple, direct language.
8. Do check facts, figures and spelling.
9. Do ensure that format and layout are correct.
10. Do choose good paper and a suitable envelope.

The top 10 don'ts
1. Don't write if a visit or phone call is better.
2. Don't send a reply while angry or annoyed.
3. Don't dictate letters unnecessarily.
4. Don't use jargon or abbreviations unless the recipient is certain to understand them.
5. Don't be either too formal or too familiar.
6. Don't pad.
7. Don't choose words or language just to impress.
8. Don't use strong or offensive language.
9. Don't use words whose meaning you are unsure of.
10. Don't sign a letter you have not checked.

Chapter 8

Reports and Brochures

Reports

For some people, writing reports causes more distress than any other part of their job. Many of us avoid reading them as long as we can, hiding them in a drawer or at the bottom of the in-tray. However, reports are often unavoidable, and can have an important, sometimes a crucial role. We must come to terms with them.

In fact, producing a good report can give as much lasting satisfaction as anything we are called on to do. We can look back on it, now and in years to come, and perhaps revel in the memory of what it achieved.

Writing a well-constructed and readable report is not as difficult as we may fear. If we do it frequently, we will soon evolve our own approach. As newcomers, or if we only write reports occasionally, a methodical approach can help to lessen the problems. Here is one:

- establish the aim
- list the main subject headings
- jot down ideas, data and subheadings
- carry out additional research
- write a first draft
- structure the draft
- work through as many redrafts as are needed
- check and edit the final draft in detail
- produce in final form.

We may move back and forth between steps several times, as our thoughts develop, but each step must eventually be covered.

Establish the aim
We may have been given clear instructions as to what our report must cover, in the form of a remit or terms of reference from our boss, a committee or other body. There may be standing instructions as to what it must cover, as is frequently the case with failure, accident and

laboratory reports. But if none of these apply, our first task is to define what we are trying to do.

The 'aim' is the key change we wish to bring about in the real world. The more closely we can define this, the better chance we have of succeeding. The act of writing down the aim will force us to think clearly and commit ourselves.

Typical aims for reports might be:

1. *To make a full and accurate record of the accident that happened in the works this morning, which can be used for insurance, legal, disciplinary or preventative action as necessary.*

2. *To record the conference committee's plan for the next annual conference and its recommendations for decision and action.*

List the main subject headings

It is best to write each possible subject heading at the top of a separate sheet. This enables us to change the order or add other headings, gives us plenty of room to scribble and the chance to insert extra sheets at any point.

The headings for the reports mentioned above might be:

1. *What actually happened*
   — *Damage resulting*
   — *The injuries to Bob Smith and Peter Brown*
   — *The action taken at the time*
   — *How the plant is being kept working until full repairs are completed*
   — *The cause*
   — *Recommendations to prevent a recurrence*

2. *Available dates and locations*
   — *Format*
   — *Possible speakers*
   — *Publicity*
   — *Costings*

Jot down ideas, data and subheadings

The key word for this step is 'jot'. If we wait for inspiration we might wait for ever. We should consider the headings we have produced with several actions in mind:

Put in the easy bits

One or two main headings often seem to write themselves; we know what we want to say and have the facts to support it at our fingertips.

Some ideas will probably be clear in our minds, though we may not be sure where they will lead, or how to link them to others. Even if we are not certain of the words of a quote, or have forgotten the source of some figures, we should note down what we remember and check later.

Scrap unnecessary headings

Other main headings will gather nothing below them. We may decide that we have to work harder on these, or that some are not valid. In the latter case, we can scrap them or combine them with other main headings.

Add or split headings

It can become clear that new main headings need to be added, or that existing headings need splitting into two or more new ones.

Rearrange

The thought may be more logical, or the report easier to read, if the order of the headings is changed. If headings and their supporting notes are written on separate sheets, rearrangement presents no problem, and the order can remain fluid for a while yet.

Generate ideas

We need as many ideas and as much material to work on as possible; we must keep ideas flowing at all costs. Negative thinking and criticism must be held at bay.

This is the heart of report writing, and because it is creative we must not restrict it. Some people find it helpful to keep pencil and paper beside their bed, even though flashes of inspiration in the early hours may infuriate their partner. Others find a pocket dictating machine helpful, despite the raised eyebrows of fellow-travellers on the 0815. Yet others disappear for an hour into an empty office away from callers and phones. The process can take anything from hours to weeks, depending on the time available and the difficulty of the task.

This step will probably produce a sheaf of untidy, scribbled pages, with crossings out, marginal additions, altered order and gaps for later material. Neither the words used, the quality of the handwriting, the grammar nor the spelling matter. Purity and correctness come later.

Carry out additional research

Report writing is often the last stage of an assignment or task, or is carried out after an event. However, the steps already completed may show that we do not have all the data, or that some aspects of our subject are not fully explored.

Gaps may not become apparent until we attempt to write a first draft, but whenever it happens, work must be interrupted while we complete the necessary research. A well-written report is *not* an effective vehicle for hiding ignorance; on the contrary, the better written it is, the clearer the depth of knowledge and thought on which it is based will be.

Write a first draft

The first draft will be based on the framework of main headings and supporting thoughts and data which we have created so far.

Getting started

For many people, starting a draft is, physically, the biggest barrier of all; they sit, pen in hand or word processor at the ready, frozen with something close to terror. However, once the hands have started moving purposefully, much of this feeling evaporates.

Two approaches can help:

The easiest heading. One approach is to go straight for the easiest heading. We have already produced our provisional structure, so the order we write the headings up in a first draft does not matter.

The gradual focus. A second way of getting started is to begin writing literally anything, and focus on the subject as we write. This may sound odd, but is akin to the technique of interviewing which aims to establish a flow by getting the interviewee talking on *anything*, and gradually focusing the conversation on the matter in hand.

Use a word processor if possible

A word processor is the ideal implement for this and the remaining stages. It enables us to draft freely in the knowledge that we can edit, rearrange, add and reject what we have written quickly and easily.

A secretary using a word processor rather than a typewriter is also able to make alterations with far less trouble.

Know when to stop

Just as a fully relaxed interviewee goes on talking too long, there is a danger that we will carry on writing past the point when we have said all that needs saying.

It is easier to cut writing down than to add to it, and the result is more likely to be elegant and well-written. But it is better still to realise when we have said enough, and to have the self-control to stop at that point.

Structure the draft

Even a short report written in a continuous flow of text, like a chapter in a book, is discouraging to the reader. People feel lost in the mass of words and are reluctant to start reading. A dense layout also makes the report harder to understand; readers may fail to follow the argument, or to notice when one point has ended and another begun. Remembering and referring to points will also be harder.

We must help and encourage the reader not only by having a structure, but by signposting it clearly. Some organisations have a standard report structure to which all writers are expected to conform. If ours is one of these, we must use it.

If we are free to choose, then we should start from a simple basic structure, adapting it later if necessary. A six-element structure will fit a wide range of reports, although short reports may not need all elements:

1. Title page
2. Summary
3. Table of contents
4. Body of the report
5. Appendices
6. Index

Title page
This should include:

- Title
- Subtitle (if used)
- Name(s) of writer(s) or group responsible
- Date presented
- Reference, address, telephone number, department, etc.

It may also include the remit, terms of reference or other instruction under which the report was written, *if* this is brief; if not, the following page should be used.

Choice of title. Titles can attract or put off potential readers. Also, if the report is to be filed and kept for long-term reference in a library, archive or database, we should give prominence to the key word under which we would like it to be indexed.

The title may have been decided before the report was written, or it may be our choice, in which case it is worth careful thought. It should be brief, but leave no doubt what the subject is. If these requirements pull in opposite directions, the device of title and subtitle can be used.

For example:

1. *The explosion in No 2 Shop*
   3 May 1989

2. *The Annual Conference, 1990*
   'The final report of the Conference Working Party'

Summary

This should come next so that those who do not have time to read the whole document can at least learn its main points, and will be encouraged to read what follows. It will concentrate the thinking of those who have the time or need to read it all.

Summaries should consist of short paragraphs covering each main conclusion, and preferably take up no more than one page. Although its place in the finished report is second, the summary should be written after the first draft and the rest of the work on structuring. Some people suggest that it is best written when the rest of the report has been finalised. However, writing it earlier gives us the same chance to edit and improve it as with the rest of the report.

Summaries are sometimes known as 'executive summaries' or 'cover sheets'. As cover sheets, they combine with the title page to form the top page of the report, making a suitable format for brief reports.

Table of contents

A table of contents will not be necessary unless the body of the report is longer than five or six pages.

The layout of the table should follow that of the report (see next section). If headings and subheadings are used, the latter should be indented; if sections are numbered, the numbers should precede the words, and page numbers should be given at the end of each line. For example:

1. <u>Possible dates and locations</u>	1
1.1 Dates to be avoided	1
1.2 The best part of the year	1
1.3 Choice of facilities	2
1.4 Dates available	4

The body of the report

The use of main headings at the start of the drafting process will already have done much to structure the body of the report.

If, when we produced the first draft, we added subheadings to guide the reader and aid clarity, they will signpost what we are saying and break the text into more readable chunks. For lengthy reports, a chapter structure with headings grouped together can be used.

If the writing is complex and lengthy, splitting subheadings into sub-subheadings will make it easier for the reader; however, in short and straightforward reports this would only confuse. We must exercise judgement, weighing the volume and complexity of the text against the possible confusion of too many headings.

Numbered headings make reference easier. It is usual to number subheadings within each main heading, and sub-subheadings within each subheading. For example:

2. <u>Format of the conference</u>
   2.1 *Plan of the working day*
       2.1.1 *Registration and welcome of delegates*
       2.1.2 *Keynote address and main speakers*
       2.1.3 *Track sessions*
       2.1.4 *Refreshment and meal arrangements*

While working on the structure of the report, we should check whether the breakdown into headings is logical. It is best not to have too many main headings: more than seven or eight would become confusing. If we cannot do without more we should adopt a chapter structure.

Appendices

Somehow, no report seems complete without at least one appendix. We may be tempted to add one just to appear respectable. However, although appendices are a useful device, many reports do not need them.

The value of an appendix is to clear detail out of the main discussion, so that it does not distract and discourage the reader. It is the place for lengthy tables of statistics, lists of names or references, detailed descriptions of methodology, copies of correspondence, transcripts of interviews with witnesses and similar supporting material.

Occasionally, it will be clear that the reader does not need the extra detail, and that we can eliminate it completely from the report.

Each appendix should be referenced at the appropriate point in the text.

Index

An index will only be needed for a lengthy report containing numerous factual statements. If needed, it must, of course, be constructed after the final draft, and page numbers can only be added when the rest of the layout has been completed.

Work through as many redrafts as are needed

An emergency report can be called for in a matter of hours; on the other hand, we may have the luxury of as much time as we want to polish a major report – in some cases, months.

Whichever situation we are in, the principle is the same: everything in a report is, by definition, on the record. Under even the tightest schedule, we owe it to ourselves and to the readers to ensure that the report is as accurate and well presented as possible.

The aim of this step is to focus on the bigger issues: overall content, logic, structure and readability. We shall, of course, correct any errors we spot, whether factual, grammatical, spelling or layout, but this is not the main aim now; detailed editing comes next. It is therefore best to read fairly quickly, stopping as rarely as possible, in order to get the feel and flow.

We should read with certain questions in mind:

Overall content
This must be checked by asking questions such as:

- Have I included all the main points?
- Is each point supported by the necessary data, evidence or discussion?
- Is there too much data or discussion of any point, or repetition or irrelevancy?

Logic
This must be checked by asking:

- Is the argument sound, both overall and in detail?
- Have I omitted any steps in reasoning, or any necessary evidence?

Structure
This will be checked by asking:

- Are chapters, sections and subsections properly made, or should they be further combined or split?
- Are the chapters, sections and subsections in the best order?
- Should any material be transferred to an appendix?

Readability

- Is the writing easy to read; does it carry the reader forward on a tide of interest?
- Are explanations clear and complete?
- Is there padding or unnecessary words?
- Is the language simple, direct and lively?
- Does it avoid pomposity and unnecessary jargon?
- Does it need illustrations (verbal, graphic or statistical)?

Graphics
We should also consider whether 'readability' is enough, or whether understanding and retention would be improved by adding or substituting pictures, charts, plans, graphs, maps etc for words. Visual aids also help readability by breaking up the text; pages of unbroken text are forbidding.

Statistical presentation
This is also the time to look carefully at the presentation of statistics; the layout, size and headings of tables are important to understanding.

Two valuable sources of help during this phase are time and other people.

Time. A period of inactivity can be fruitful. If we start revising as soon as we have finished drafting, our thoughts will probably run along the same channels. If we can put the draft aside for hours, days or even weeks, there is a better chance that when we do look at it again we shall see it with fresh eyes.

Other people can be an immense help, and we must never be too proud to ask them. Report writers often become so wrapped up in what they have written that they cannot see the flaws in it.

However, finding willing and helpful readers is not always easy. We will want to avoid some people for political reasons; they may be involved in the situation we are reporting on, or there may be interdepartmental, status or personal difficulties.

Readers must be people whose judgement we trust, who will say what they think and report promptly. They do not have to be subject experts; comments from lay people can be very helpful, and they often ask the simple questions that we, as experts, have not even considered.

Check and edit the final draft in detail
There comes a point when redrafting ceases to be useful. This may

Statistical graphics

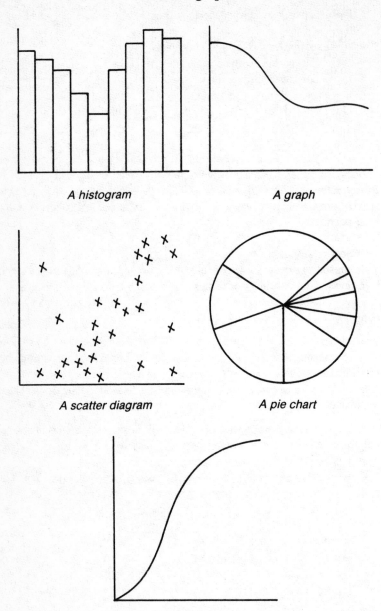

A histogram

A graph

A scatter diagram

A pie chart

Cumulative frequency curves (ogives)

come quickly, because we are running out of time, or after much thought and work, because we have exhausted our own and other people's constructive criticism.

In either case, we shall need to check and edit in detail. Nothing pleases critics more than spotting a trivial spelling mistake, misuse of a punctuation mark or an incorrectly totalled column of figures. Such errors can make us look less competent than if our major conclusions were in doubt – indeed, the latter are a matter of opinion, but a misspelling is not.

While redrafting, we should have picked up and corrected some detailed errors; we must now ensure that none have escaped. We need to check:

- spelling
- punctuation
- correct choice and use of words
- grammar
- section and page numbering
- textual omissions or duplication
- incorrect figures, writing addition, etc.

Checking, especially of our own work, is more difficult than it may seem; there is a temptation to read not what is on the page, but what should be.

The advice given in Chapter 7 (pages 131–4) will also be helpful during this stage.

Produce in final form

Management consultants who live by producing reports spend much time, skill and expense on the physical production, and so should we.

Most people, however sophisticated and professional, are as strongly impressed by the wrapping as by the contents of a parcel. The look and feel of a carefully produced document will inspire the receiver with immediate confidence. A scruffy, badly produced report will evoke a negative reaction, and is less likely to be read or believed.

Modern technology facilitates a high standard of production: word processing, graphics software, efficient reprographics and desk-top publishing are all powerful aids for the report-writer. Of course, we may have access to none of these, and our resources of time or money may not be sufficient to take advantage of them, but it is worth making quite sure before resigning ourselves to the products of a typewriter.

Whatever resources we have must be put to best use. We will need to consider:

- method of production and reproduction
- paper size and quality
- pagination and layout
- type style
- graphics and illustrations
- cover or binding.

Method of production and reproduction
Better a handwritten report that conveys the relevant information to those who need to know quickly than a printed document that is a month late.

With a word processor we can run off as many copies as we need to the highest standard our printer will produce. A laser printer produces the finest finished work and disks can increasingly be used by a commercial printer. If we have access to a desk-top publishing facility, we can add an extra touch of class, especially to title pages and graphics.

Failing such facilities (even from a bureau or subcontractor) we must beg or borrow the best typewriter we can, and produce copies by photocopying or a similar process.

Paper size and quality
We should choose the best paper our resources can stretch to. Crisp, white paper of a good weight (at least 100 gsm) is impressive to handle and has a feeling of quality. We should use a process which produces all copies on similar paper; it is not the top copy only on which we will be judged.

Paper of A4 size, used in 'portrait' format (ie the longer sides vertical) is best for most purposes, but we should consider other possibilities. The smaller A5 size is easier to carry, and paper used in 'landscape' format (ie the longer sides horizontal) can be better for graphics, illustrations or statistical tables.

Pagination and layout
It is impressive to allow plenty of space in a report. Starting each main section on a fresh page and allowing ample space between subsections helps to emphasise the structure, and avoid forbidding pages of unbroken text.

Even if sections are numbered, numbering of the pages is also essential for easy reference and indexing.

Type style
We should choose the best combination of type size and style for titles,

headings, subheadings and captions. If in doubt, printers can usually advise.

Graphics and illustrations

The use of graphics software for micros and desk-top publishers can enhance the appearance of a report. Many are cheap and user-friendly, and if we are not familiar with what they can do, it is worth finding out.

Illustrations, plans, diagrams, maps, etc can be drawn and reproduced easily on modern equipment. Even photographs can now be reproduced satisfactorily, at least in black and white, by modern copiers.

Cover or binding

A report will always look better with a cover, even if it is no more than a neat title page. If the report is large, a stiff and attractive cover will enhance its appearance, and keep it in good condition during use.

Even the simplest report must have some way of keeping the pages in the right order and ensuring they stay that way. Stapling is satisfactory for reports of a few pages; transparent plastic with a plastic slider to grip the sheets looks neat and impressive, but may not hold sheets firmly by itself. For longer reports, special equipment may be called for; comb binding or heat sealing are frequently used.

Brochures

There is a large and important class of written productions designed to communicate limited amounts of information to a fairly closely defined readership. They include: leaflets, handbooks, manuals, programmes, circulars, pamphlets, catalogues, handbills and brochures. For convenience, all these will be called 'brochures' in what follows.

Handbooks and instruction leaflets designed to help customers who have purchased goods are particularly important and frequently neglected. But unless customers know how to use correctly what they have bought, they will ultimately be less satisfied; there is no point in providing features which remain unused, or in failing to do everything possible to avoid misuse. This fault is especially common among suppliers of computer and other electronic products, who frequently underestimate the help needed by their customers.

The process of producing brochures is similar in many respects to report writing. We must also always ensure the following steps are covered:

- define the target readership

- list the headings
- decide the best order of headings
- fill in the detail under each heading
- consider illustrations, type size and layout
- revise and edit
- arrange production.

Define the target readership
The more closely we can define the likely readership the more effective the brochure will be. We should ask questions such as:

- What will attract their attention to the brochure?
- What do they already know about the subject?
- What is their general background?
- How is the brochure likely to reach them?

List the headings
The headings will outline the answer to the question:

- What are the items of information we want readers to learn from the brochure?

Apart from information directly relevant to the main subject, it is often appropriate to add general information about our organisation or operation.

We can often get help from other brochures designed to do the same or a similar job; last year's conference programme; brochures about similar products; brochures for the previous round of recruitment and so on. In using such examples, we must check how successful the previous brochure was and how it could have been improved in use. If we produce such items regularly, we should make notes on these aspects.

If the brochure is to carry advertisements for other organisations, products or services, provision must be made for them at this stage.

Decide the best order of headings
The order must work to gain the reader's attention, guide him through any introductory material and help him to select from those items where he has a choice. We may choose an order based on time or date sequence, following a process (such as setting up and operating equipment), price, function, location, or an alphabetical or numerical order.

By the end, the reader must have no doubt what action we want him to take. If appropriate, we must provide clear instructions or perhaps an order form.

Complete the detail under each heading

We must ensure that all necessary information is provided, asking: what information must the reader have to make full use of what this brochure describes?

For many brochures, such information will include specifications or descriptions (possibly with pictures, plans or other illustrations), dates, places, prices, booking details, contact names, addresses and telephone numbers.

Brochures often have a number of repetitive sections: the pieces in a concert programme; the books in a publisher's catalogue; the products in a sales brochure; the courses in a college prospectus. It saves time, improves the layout and helps readers if we design a standard format which can be used for each category of items.

Here again, the previous example – if there was one – can often save work, but we must ensure that all information is fully up to date, accurate and suitable for the job in hand.

Consider illustrations, type size and layout

Illustrations will add interest and aid communication in almost any brochure. They will also add to costs, not only by the cost of production, but also by the extra space they will occupy. The final decision will usually depend on the budget.

Good layout is essential to an effective brochure. The facilities offered by desk-top publishing make in-house layout design more practicable, or we may decide to use the services of a professional layout artist. These can be obtained through a printer or advertising agency, or by employing a freelance.

Layout is an art form requiring considerable skill, but hints can be gained from the design of similar and successful brochures. It can help to produce mock-ups by cutting and pasting material from other leaflets and typescript. The process will be easier if we have access to a copier with enlarging and reduction facilities, and the mock-up can be further enhanced by using transfer lettering for headings.

An early decision will be the page size. This will depend on the way the brochure is to be used, whether it needs to match other paperwork, the means of production and the budget available. Throughout we must consider the design from the angle of the user, and above all avoid muddle and overcrowding.

Blank sides of paper are effectively wasted assets and can usually be put to good use.

Revise and edit the complete brochure
This work is similar to the same steps in producing a report (see pages 149–51).

Arrange production
Brochures will usually be printed, or at least reproduced, to the highest quality we can afford.

The employment of a printer will necessitate giving a clear brief. If we are using the services of an agency, it will choose and brief the printer on our behalf, but we must keep in close touch with what is being done and ensure it is what we require.

In briefing a printer direct, we will need to decide paper weight, quality and finish; type faces and sizes; and the number of colours (from one to full four-colour work) we require. Samples of paper, type and colour should all be provided for us. We must also decide what length of print-run we need, and check delivery dates and details.

It is essential to see at least one proof and to check it thoroughly. If colour is involved, we will need a colour proof, and it may be necessary to have special proofs of the cover if this involves different materials, colours or processes. This stage should not be used to re-edit the material as, apart from causing delay, author's corrections in proof incur extra charges.

Report and brochure writing – the top 20

The top 10 dos
1. Do ensure your aims and objectives are clear.
2. Do write draft headings on separate sheets of paper.
3. Do establish the best order of headings from the reader's point of view.
4. Do produce a tight, comprehensive and logical structure.
5. Do write the easy bits first.
6. Do produce a first, rough draft quickly.
7. Do use charts, graphs, plans and pictures freely.
8. Do allow as much time as possible for maturation.
9. Do seek the views of others.
10. Do check facts, figures, spelling and all other details thoroughly.

The top 10 don'ts

1. Don't wait for inspiration to strike.
2. Don't mix creative and critical thinking.
3. Don't flannel or try to hide ignorance; find out.
4. Don't pad.
5. Don't try to impress for its own sake.
6. Don't clutter the body of the report with detail.
7. Don't use long sections of unbroken text.
8. Don't use long or complex sentences.
9. Don't skimp on the final physical production.
10. Don't leave anything to chance; check at every stage.

Chapter 9

News Releases
and Advertising

As noted in Chapter 6, communication with and through the media includes news releases and advertising. These are now considered.

News releases

A news release is a short written statement on a subject produced for issue to and used by the media.

The receiving media can choose to: ignore the release (as happens to the majority); use it in an edited form for a small item; use it as written; contact the issuer and add material to produce a longer report; incorporate or comment on the release in editorial form.

The treatment a release will get depends on several factors including:

- intrinsic interest
- choice of recipients
- style and language
- format
- timing.

Intrinsic interest

It is difficult to make bricks without straw. In the desire to achieve free coverage, many organisations issue 'releases' which are no more than thinly disguised advertising. Such releases may be used by trade and specialist journals who are desperate for copy, but have otherwise little hope in life.

What will be regarded as 'news' of sufficient interest to be reported depends on the market, interests and beliefs of the journal, and its reporters. For success, we must know what these are. It will also depend on what other news is available at the same time, and to that extent is outside our control.

The kinds of event that may stand a chance include:

- disasters, accidents, fires, mishaps
- crime
- strikes, lockouts, working-to-rule
- bankruptcy, receivership and major financial problems
- unexpected or interesting research or survey results
- the expression of controversial opinion
- changes in top or well-known personnel
- new products or product ranges
- big orders or contracts
- major new buildings or equipment
- relocation
- heavy recruitment or redundancies.

Whether we seek advantage from the less fortunate items on the list must be a matter of fine judgement. All publicity is not always good publicity, but as bad news usually gets out, we may gain more by taking the initiative than by leaving it to others to set the pace.

Such a list, amplified from our own circumstances and experience, should always be available and checked to ensure that opportunities for publicity are not missed.

It is sometimes possible to lift a weak item by the choice of angle. This is discussed in the section 'Style and language', page 161.

The choice of recipients

We must consider not only where we would like our release to be published (to which our answer might well be 'as widely as possible'), but where it is most likely to be of interest. In thinking about this, it is useful to classify media. A working classification is:

- national newspapers, radio and TV
- local newspapers and radio, and regional TV
- broad interest magazines and journals
- specialist magazines and journals.

Each of these has different needs and is attracted by different material. Few releases would be suitable for use within more than one category.

National newspapers, radio and TV
Examples are the *Independent*, the *Daily Mail*, the *Sun*, the *Observer*; BBC Radio 4, ITN. These look mainly for items of national interest and

importance, irrespective of subject. They may, depending on the volume of other material available, use items which, while of narrower intrinsic interest or less importance, have an angle they see as of particular interest to their own readership, or supporting their own beliefs.

In producing releases for newspapers in this category, we must bear in mind the political platform of the paper and the profile of its readership.

Local newspapers and radio, and regional TV

The *Derby Evening Telegraph*, *Yorkshire Evening Press*, BBC Radio Leicester, Radio Trent and Border Television are examples. Strong local interest is the key to these media. Any item which offers this will be looked on with favour; those which do not, however otherwise interesting or important, are very unlikely to be used.

This category includes many free-issue papers. These prefer items from those who buy advertising space, but will normally use good local material from any source to fill the space available.

Broad interest magazines and journals

The Economist, the *Spectator* and *Nature* are journals in this category; they mainly use news items within their special area of interest (eg the national economic scene; the national political scene; developments in the natural sciences etc) which are of national importance. However, because of the breadth of these interests and the many aspects each covers, suitably angled releases on a range of subjects will be considered, provided they appear of sufficient importance.

Specialist magazines and journals

Building, *Power Farming*, *Brewing and Distilling International* are examples. This large category includes trade and professional journals; sport and hobby magazines (eg *Autocar*, the *Cricketer*, the *Railway Magazine*); academic, learned and technical journals (eg the *Architects' Journal*, *Bulletin of Hispanic Studies*, *Modern Language Review*); magazines of local interest (eg the *Dalesman*, *Derbyshire Life* and *Countryside*) and many others.

Business news releases are most likely to interest appropriate trade and professional journals, but may also attract suitable sport, hobby or other special interest magazines. It is particularly important to study the journals which we believe could be interested.

The best sources of media titles and addresses are *British Rate and Data* and *Pims Media Directory* (published monthly) and *Willings Press Guide* and the *Writers' and Artists' Yearbook* (published annually).

In every category, we must remember that journalists from editor down are human, with the usual range of interests and biases; the more we know about these, the better chance our release will have. We must study the paper carefully and, if we have time, make direct contact with editorial staff.

Style and language
All the guidelines for effective written communication discussed in other chapters apply, plus the following specific points:

The most important message first
The need to grab the attention, first of the journalist, then of the reader, is paramount. A good headline will help to achieve this, even though it is unlikely to be used by the journal.

Releases are invariably edited from the bottom upwards, so we must make our statements in order of importance. This may mean placing the most striking statement out of context right at the start, beginning with a provocative quotation, or even twisting the order of words within the first sentence.

For example, a release written in purely logical order, might be:

Three well-known professional trainers have, after careful consideration, decided to form a partnership designed to provide a training service for small businesses. The service will concentrate on skills and knowledge of immediate, practical application, such as bookkeeping, tax regulations, employment law, and the use of micros and word processors.

By beginning with the most striking statement, we could produce the following:

'Instant application is the must for successful training,' according to Peter Jones, one of three well-known professional trainers who have decided to set up a new training partnership. 'Business people who are on the road to success in smaller businesses only have time for training they can apply at once,' he said today.

The partnership will concentrate on offering courses on bookkeeping, tax regulations, employment law, and the use of micros and word processors, subjects which they believe are of immediate value to recently established businesses . . .

Matched style
If we hope to see our releases used prominently and unedited, we will need a close feel for the style of the journals we want to use them. A

release, ideal for use by the *Church Times*, would need rewriting for the *Sunday People*. There is no short cut to this knowledge, which calls for regular and analytical reading of the journals concerned.

Of course, if our aim is blanket coverage, we must adopt a generally acceptable and easily adaptable style.

Angle

An uninteresting event can be made into an effective release by the choice of an unusual angle. 'Human interest' is the most popular, followed by mysteries and the unexplained. Failing these, a lead-in incorporating little-known facts or a link with current news items and public preoccupations may lift a release from the pedestrian to the outstanding.

For example, a purely factual release might say:

Midas's new range of gnomes
Midas International today launched their latest product, a self-destructing plastic gnome. The gnome is available in a range of colours and sizes to suit all pockets, and poses include the waving gnome, the weeping gnome, the fishing gnome and the gnome-in-the-wheelbarrow.

Human interest. A human interest approach to the same event could result in a release such as:

Maggy Smith pulls it off
Maggy Smith today realised a lifelong ambition, when she pulled the lever to produce the very first of Midas International's new range of plastic gnomes. Maggy, 59 and married with two grown-up sons, has worked in the Midas factory for 38 years, but until today had never actually made a gnome. 'It was a real thrill,' she said afterwards. The foreman, Bert Jones, commented, 'She still has a bit to learn, but with practice she could do a really good job.' Launched today, the range includes colours and sizes to suit all pockets, and comes in all popular poses.

Mysteries and the unexplained. This angle might result in something like:

The mystery of the disappearing gnome
Can plastic gnomes come alive? was the question being asked at Midas International today, as the company set about solving the mystery of the disappearing gnome. The missing gnome was one of Midas's brand new range, which includes colours and sizes to suit all pockets. Besides fishing gnomes, all popular poses are available.

'We produced 50 fishing gnomes last night,' said Bert Jones, works foreman, 'ready for today's launch of the new range. I counted them myself, and we locked

up, just as we always do. This morning when I opened up, there were only 49. You could have knocked me down with a feather!'

Managing Director Alistair Smoothtalk commented, 'We have never experienced anything like this before. Our gnomes are certainly lifelike, but we didn't know they could actually walk away.'

This approach must have at least some basis in fact if it is to stand up to the inevitable probing.

The little-known fact. A little-known fact, which would attract the trade if not the general press might be:

<u>*Gnome's one-in-a-million nose*</u>
Arthur, a kneeling gnome made by Midas International for their new range launched today, has a nose in a million. In fact, according to Bert Jones, Midas works foreman, Arthur has a one in 1,234,876 nose. Bert explains:

'People don't generally realise that a gnome's nose is not made in one piece. In fact, it has three pieces, cunningly jointed where you can't see unless you look very carefully. But we decided to try and do it in one, and Arthur's nose is the result. We don't know what he thinks about it, but we're all absolutely delighted.'

The new range includes colours and sizes to suit all pockets, and comes in all popular poses.

A link with current news and public preoccupations would suggest:

<u>*The environmentally friendly gnome has arrived*</u>
'There are now millions of unwanted gnomes in the rubbish dumps of this country which will outlast our civilisation. Plastic gnomes that self-destruct at the end of 20 years will make a major contribution to the environment,' said Alistair Smoothtalk, Managing Director of Midas International yesterday. 'Indestructible plastic has been used for too long,' he said. 'Our new range will never outlive their welcome.'

The range of environmentally friendly gnomes from Midas includes colours and sizes to suit all pockets, and comes in all popular poses . . .

Format
The format of a news release will affect its chances of success, and attention to detail is worthwhile. We need to consider the addressee, our identification, and the date and time of release:

The addressee
If we have individual contacts, or know the names of journalists who

will be interested, then we should address the release to them. Names can often be picked up by reading the journal concerned. Failing a name, we should select the most relevant job title. For newspapers, radio and TV, the best addressee for general releases is the News Editor. Specialised releases can be sent to the Industrial, Political or Sports Editor, etc as appropriate.

Identification

A news release must specify the name, address and telephone number of the issuer and the person who can be contacted for further information. Because journalists work odd hours, it is best to use a telephone that is manned 24 hours a day. If this is not possible, both work and home numbers should be given.

Date and time of release

If possible, releases should be issued some days before we wish them to be used. This gives recipients the opportunity to raise queries or seek amplification and allows for postal delay. If radio or television are involved, it gives sufficient time for interviews to be arranged.

However, to ensure the news is not leaked out in dribs and drabs, we should *embargo* the release. This is done simply by stating on it that it is 'Embargoed until . . .' or 'For release at . . .' It is important to state a time as well as a date, to avoid any possible doubt with editions and late-night news bulletins.

Journalists invariably respect such embargoes, as not to do so would result in their being denied hot news thereafter, and cause conflict with their colleagues.

The timing

The timing of a news release is critical.

If our release hits the newsdesk within minutes of news of a major plane crash or the sudden death of a pop star, we will be lucky to get a couple of column centimetres, and if we do, we will be even luckier to be noticed by readers.

Acts of God apart, the optimum timing for the majority of releases should be planned with care. We must consider what other events may be in the diaries of the journalists we wish to interest. Budget or Derby day, a test match at Lords, Wimbledon, the CBI or TUC conference etc.

We should also consider the days of the week or year on which news is likely to be scarcest. A release that is passed over on a Friday in September may make the lead story on a Saturday in August.

Finally, we must keep a weather eye on the competition, and if it makes a move that might queer our pitch, we must move even faster. The one who gets his release out first will scoop the coverage.

A sample of a press release for this book is given below.

PRESS RELEASE

By Carrier Pigeon or Computer, Wax Tablet or Telephone, our ability to communicate effectively is essential to our survival . . . according to Malcolm Peel, author of the second fully revised edition of **Improving Your Communication Skills**, published by Kogan Page.

'Our ability to communicate' explains Peel 'is among our most important life skills. The more effectively we communicate, the better our chances in every aspect of life.'

Malcolm Peel examines every form of communication, from meetings and interview techniques through writing skills to coping with the latest in communication technology.

Using a practical and straightforward approach based on well-tried methods and personal experience, he explains how we can vastly improve our range of communication techniques.

How, for instance, during a presentation, a picture really can be worth a thousand words.

Or the several different ways in which a potentially embarrassing subject can be broached smoothly and satisfactorily in a face-to-face discussion.

With examples of effective and non-effective communication in everyday business situations, this book is a highly practical, methodical and lively guide for self-improvement.

Please see over for further details

The Author

Malcolm Peel's career has included experience of all aspects of business communication. He has conducted many courses in communication and is the author of *Customer Service, How to Make Meetings Work* and *Readymade Interview Questions*, all published by Kogan Page. He is currently Head of Consultancy and Advisory Services with the Institute of Management.

Improving Your Communication Skills

2nd edition, fully revised

Malcolm Peel

Publication date: 24 February 1995

£9.99 Paperback   ISBN 0 7494 1542 8
224 pages   216mm × 135mm

Available from good bookshops or direct from the publisher (please enclose 10% postage and packing)

Kogan Page, 120 Pentonville Road, Islington, London N1 9JN   Telephone: 0171-278 0433

MALCOLM PEEL IS AVAILABLE FOR INTERVIEW FROM 1 FEBRUARY 1995.

FOR A REVIEW COPY OR FOR FURTHER INFORMATION PLEASE CONTACT LISA DAY ON 0171-278 0433.

Advertising

Advertising is attempted communication to a number of individually unknown people designed to influence them, usually to buy something or accept a point of view. It can use all media and any means of communication, from sandwich boards to skywriting.

It is a field in which vast sums are spent and tens of thousands employed. It generates strong feelings: some see it as the motor of a healthy economy, others as harmful, even immoral. Whatever view we take, it is impossible to deny that it involves highly effective communication.

Advertising tends to be the domain of specialists, and most organisations that spend heavily on it use an agency. For the smaller organisation, it is impossible to do more here than indicate questions that should be asked and suggest how answers may be found.

Points to consider regarding advertising are:

- whether to advertise
- how much to spend
- whether to use an agency
- which media to use
- production of the advertisements
- measuring the results.

Whether to advertise

There are several potential uses for advertising:

To sell

Advertising is an obvious choice for anyone who has something to sell. Unless we are selling as much as we would like, and are confident we shall continue to do so into the foreseeable future, advertising must be on the agenda.

Corporate advertising

Advertising may be considered for purposes other than direct selling. Corporate advertising aims to strengthen and improve the overall image of an organisation or a product. Even less directly, it may be used to raise the general level of consciousness and knowledge of an industry or economic sector.

Propaganda

Advertising may be used to persuade people that our views are correct or that the views held by others are wrong.

To buy

As well as a selling aid, advertising can help us when we wish to buy. This is especially true in a buyers' market, or when matching buyer and seller is difficult, perhaps for geographical reasons. The most common use in buying situations is for filling job vacancies.

Alternatives to advertising

Whether advertising is the best way of achieving our objectives can be difficult to foresee. There are usually alternatives: face-to-face contact, if it can be arranged, is often the most effective method, whether we are filling a managerial post by headhunting, or selling plastic food containers at parties. In fact, advertising is often best used to supplement other methods of communication.

How much to spend

Advertising can be one of the most expensive activities undertaken by an organisation. Some organisations, on the other hand, spend little or nothing.

The cost of placement is only part of the total, whether for a campaign or a single advertisement. There are also the costs of copy-writing, artwork and production. The only certain rule must be to get maximum value for every pound spent.

We will need to consider whether our objectives can be met by single advertisements, or whether we must plan a campaign. Much advertising relies on reinforcement of its message by constant repetition and the use of several media (eg TV, press and posters). In this situation, ten times the expenditure may yield 50 times the result. But a campaign will often call for many advertisements and the use of several different media over a prolonged period; a massive expenditure for which the return can never be certainly foreseen.

There are other situations in which economy is self-defeating: a small advertisement for a senior vacancy, for example, may prove of no value at all.

Whether to use an agency

Many people feel a need for professional advice when considering large advertising expenditure and this is readily available from an advertising agency. Advertising agencies have gained great presence in recent decades, and now assume a major role even in general election campaigns. They have also made large fortunes for many people, and their advice can rarely be totally disinterested.

A competent agency will have the knowledge and skills to understand our needs and to advise us on or conduct market research. It will be well placed to advise on the overall strategy, the best timing and most effective choice of media. It will have the resources to create appropriate images in words or pictures and to make the best use of the chosen media. It will undertake all aspects of the planning, design and copy-writing.

However, this expertise can be costly. If our needs are straightforward or our resources limited, it may be better to rely on our own skills, possibly reinforced by professional help in one or two areas.

The competence of advertising agencies varies from superb to appalling. There are also agencies of virtually every size, and some which specialise in particular market segments or types of work. Agency staff are also mobile, and the loss or acquisition of one or two talented individuals can have an immense effect on their success. It pays to shop around and to continually review possibilities even after successful experience of a particular agency.

Which media to use

The range of available media is almost endless, including: books, periodicals, newspapers, brochures, leaflets, circulars, radio, television, posters, exhibitions, sandwich boards, skywriting and many others.

The choice (and we may decide to use several as part of the same campaign) will depend on our budget, whether we can identify our target market and what that market is.

Studies of national advertising campaigns have suggested that an overall ranking of response per pound spent, from high to low, is: cinema, TV, radio, telephone, poster, print. This list does not apply, however, to local advertising.

Of more practical importance is detailed knowledge of the best media for particular products, services and situations. In many cases the choice of media will be limited by convention and the expectations of the market in which we wish to sell. A conference, a vacancy for a works accountant, a seaside excursion and a ladies' hair salon are each likely to require different media for best results.

The subdivisions of product (or service) and media are both important. Different types of conference and different job vacancies will call for different media. We must consider not only whether to use newspapers rather than brochures, but which newspapers; not only whether to use TV, but which channels, which days and what times. The subdivisions of 'print', for example, include:

- newspaper advertising

- journal advertising
- Yellow Pages
- inserts
- direct mail
- brochures.

Only experience will show which, or which combination, is best for us. We must experiment and monitor the results.

Design and production of the advertisements

The design and wording of an advertisement can rarely be considered in isolation. It will frequently be one of a series, or part of an extended campaign. It must also contribute to the overall image of the organisation, through the use of a consistent 'house style'.

A house style is developed by the use of a logo, consistent type-faces, standard design features such as framing and layout, possibly colour, and to a smaller extent by the use of words.

For anything more ambitious than an insert in the classified column of an evening paper, effective advertising will require a considerable range of skills, including visualising, drawing, animation, copy-writing, photography, and typesetting.

We may have these skills ourselves or within our organisation; the availability of computerised aids such as desk-top publishing has vastly extended the range of what can be done in-house. But if we do not, or if we have doubts, we should call in professional assistance. Some journals and newspapers will provide design and copy-writing services, although others expect us to provide 'camera ready' advertisements.

Measuring the response

In theory, it ought to be possible to measure the results of advertising, but in practice this is difficult. While the results of one-off advertisements (eg for job vacancies) can be measured, to spend large sums on campaigns and background advertising must always be at least partly an act of faith.

The response to specific advertisements can be monitored by the use of reply coupons (coded to indicate which media they have come from) or additions to the reply address (eg 'Department DM3'). But if responses come by telephone, letter, company order form, or through people who were told of the advertisement by someone else, replies are difficult to classify. Unless the product (or whatever is being offered) has not previously been advertised, it will also be difficult to eliminate responses from previous advertisements and other sources.

Advertising Feature: A Wyvern Business Library Recommendation. Practical problem solving books for busy managers.

How to break into high income consulting

Demand for good consultants is growing at a phenomenal rate. Could you cash in on this highly lucrative market

Have you, like many middle and senior managers, built up a goldmine of expertise over the years? Expertise that other companies would be willing to pay handsomely to share?

Successful consultants should expect to earn at least double to three times the salaried rate for their work - once they are established.

Why?

For every company that can afford your expertise full time, there are scores of others who need you for a limited period. They can justify paying many times the salaried rate because they avoid the cost and commitment of permanent employment.

They are paying for the extremely concentrated and focused expertise a skilled professional consultant can bring into their company.

Control your own destiny

How many people do you know who have gone back to a salaried job after tasting the freedom of being self employed?

No permanent office politics. No staff problems. If you want to take four holidays a year who is to say no? Once established you should be able to afford it. Or you can choose to work 7 days a week and 'rake it in'.

You choose when you want to work and for whom you work. But above all you have the freedom to control your own destiny.

Essential know-how

High Income Consulting gives you the information, the techniques, the know-how to break into a top paying profession.

It shows you how to make the successful move from "employee" to consultant -

running your own profitable business.

It's all here. How to set and get the fees you want. How to get up to 80% repeat and referral business. How to get your business plan together. How to set retainer fees (regular safe income). How to collect your cash.

As you read you will be able to decide whether you already have the expertise and temperament to become a successful highly paid consultant. Armed with this book you will also have the know-how.

High Income Consulting 316 pages
Hardback £25.00 + p&p*. Coupon below

THE SMALL PRINT. Guarantee: If you return your book(s) and Receipt within 10 days of receipt, we will refund your money in full without question. You do NOT have to buy a set number of books. This is in addition to your statutory rights. **Free mailing list service:** by ordering a book you will join this service. We keep you informed of our own products and services and we encourage other organisations to mail their offers to selections of our mailing list. If you don't want this full service please write "Exclude from third party mailings" across the coupon.

Wyvern Business ✦ Library	Wyvern Business Library Tel: 01353 665544 A division of Wyvern Crest Ltd., 6 The Business Park, Ely, Cambs. CB7 4JW	NO QUIBBLE MONEY BACK GUARANTEE

To: Wyvern Business Library, FREEPOST CB 511, Ely, Cambs CB7 4BR (No stamp needed.)

YES! Please send me **High Income Consulting** at £27.95 (£25.00 + £2.95 p&p)

☐ I enclose my cheque made payable to Wyvern Business Library for £ ....

Please debit my ☐ ▨ ☐ ▨ ☐ ▨ ☐ ▨ ☐ E   Expires ..../.........

Card No. ☐☐☐☐ ☐☐☐☐ ☐☐☐☐ ☐☐☐☐

Name Mr/Ms .... Signed ....

Position ....

Company ....

Address (inc postcode) ....

....

*P&P UK: Add £2.95 for one book, £3.95 for two or more books.
Overseas: £4.50 for one book, £7.50 for two or more.

PRIORITY ORDERS
☎ 01353 665544
Fax:
01353 667666
24 hours, every day.
Use your credit card.
Quote ref PU8.

Comparisons between periods with and without advertising are also difficult and an unreliable measure. The response to advertising may be delayed, and other factors at work can include the general economic climate, the success of competitors, and customers' experience of the product. However, in the 1970s *American Business Press* compared companies' sales with advertising expenditure during the 1974–75 recession, and found that companies which did not cut back on advertising did better in the long run. By 1977, companies which had cut back their advertising had increased sales by 50 per cent, but those which had not cut back had *doubled* their sales.

What goes into a printed advertisement?

Illustration
If there is an illustration, the reader's eye goes to it first. From there to the headline, and thence to copy. Photographs carry more credibility than drawings.

Headline
Five times as many people read the headline as read the copy. Long headlines are read more than short ones. Four times as many people read headlines that promise benefits, for example:

**Up to 12.5% interest on your instantly accessible
savings account**

Copy
More people remember advertisements that contain news or include the price. People will read long copy, provided it is interesting. Always tell the reader what action to take: ask him to buy now, phone, call, fill in a coupon.

News releases and advertising – the top 20

The top 10 dos
1. Do review all aspects of your operation regularly to ensure opportunities for publicity are not missed.
2. Do study media carefully when considering news releases or promotional articles.
3. Do choose the most effective angle to news when writing releases.
4. Do place key statements at the start of a news release.

5. Do check all statements in news releases, articles and books for complete accuracy.
6. Do consider the optimum timing for news releases and articles.
7. Do send news releases out in advance, embargoed to an appropriate date and time.
8. Do make your headline offer a benefit wherever possible. It has to grab the reader's attention.
9. Do ensure that body copy in your advertisements interests and informs the reader, and tells him what action to take.
10. Do try to evaluate the return on advertising expenditure as accurately as possible.

The top 10 don'ts

1. Don't send out a release unless you have a good story.
2. Don't issue a news release without full identifying information and a contact telephone number.
3. Don't send releases at the last moment.
4. Don't use long sentences or long paragraphs.
5. Don't overdo the use of adjectives, as it undermines credibility.
6. Don't use type-faces and colour contrasts that make your advertisements difficult to read.
7. Don't place advertisements in inappropriate printed media (a chartered accountant is not likely to read the *Sun*).
8. Don't expect a full page advertisement to produce twice the number of responses as a half-page; the actual increase is likely to be nearer 70 per cent.
9. Don't overlook the use of inserts in magazines.
10. Don't underestimate the costs of effective advertising.

Part 3

Communication Technology

Chapter 10

The Telephone

The telephone is today one of the principal means of business communication, without which many operations would be impossible. Its importance seems likely to grow for many years to come, with the increasing use of mobile telephones and other continuing improvements in technology.

However, the telephone is also a source of problems and failures in communication and its effective use requires skill and care. A single poorly handled telephone call can ruin years of selling effort.

Over the course of time, many people develop a good telephone technique, and are able to convey a subtle and controlled message. They may find they can hide their feelings more easily than when confronting someone face to face. Some even find it easier to convey difficult or unpleasant messages by telephone, because they are less distracted by the hearer's reactions. Others do not develop a technique so quickly, and benefit from self-analysis and training.

It is worth looking at the telephone's distinctive characteristics, reviewing our own techniques and level of skill, and ensuring that we are up to date with the technology.

We can think of the use of the telephone under seven headings:

- distinctive characteristics
- making a call
- receiving a call
- transferring a call
- taking a message
- the secretary
- special equipment.

Distinctive characteristics

The telephone is deceptively simple, but has a character of its own, and communicating by phone has important differences from talking face to face. These include:

The voice

The telephone communicates by sound alone. If the sound is misunderstood, there is no body language to help put things right. We cannot modify a poorly chosen word by a smile, and if we sound aggressive, sarcastic or impatient, there is no friendly gesture to soften the impression. The hearer will be put off by too loud a voice, and if we speak too quietly or too quickly he must interrupt and tell us so, introducing tension into both sides of the conversation.

The voice, therefore, must convey a great deal. It alone can indicate that we are warm, friendly, alert and want to communicate effectively with the person at the other end of the line. If it transmits reactions or emotions, we must be sure they are what we intend. As speakers, we must therefore take care not only with our words, but with the way we speak them.

The first few words of a phone call are even more important than when communicating face to face. If they come out badly, it will be much harder to correct a wrong impression.

Recent advice circulated by British Telecom suggests that the physical posture adopted while we are speaking on the phone can make a difference. Standing up helps to create a sense of authority, while actions such as clenching the fists, curling the toes and flattening the stomach can relieve tension. It advises those who gesture when talking face to face to do so when using the phone.

Listening

Because sound is all we have, we listen to the other party on a telephone call with more attention and sensitivity than when face to face. The telephone also exaggerates the way reactions are conveyed by the voice; the slightest hesitation, the most minute intake of breath, a lowering of tone or a speeding up of speech are immediately apparent.

Many people recognise voices quickly and easily on the phone. Accent and intonation appear more evident. People who sound like standard English speakers when face to face reveal their regional origins when we hear them on the phone: they are not speaking differently, but we are listening more acutely.

As hearers, we must avoid over-reaction and misinterpretation. If the speaker sounds aggressive, curt or angry, it may be for reasons quite unrelated to the conversation: something that happened before it began, something happening at the other end, or simply because he is nervous and untrained in using the telephone. If we fail to hear clearly, we should say so – there are no gestures or facial expressions to help.

We must also remind ourselves that an effective telephone speaker can mask his feelings more easily than when face to face.

Being overheard

As we develop telephone listening techniques, we automatically apply them even when we overhear a telephone conversation to which we are not a party.

To overhear one end of a telephone conversation often tells us more, in the absence of modifying and distracting body language, than overhearing both sides of a conversation in the same room. If, for example, we unavoidably overhear a conversation between a colleague and spouse, we will probably learn a great deal about the state of their relationship.

Apart from emphasising the power of practised telephone technique, this suggests the importance of privacy when making or receiving sensitive calls.

Silence

On the telephone, silence is usually taken to indicate a problem. If we cannot continue the conversation, perhaps because we are searching for papers or shutting the door, we should always make the reason clear.

Other conversations

As when face to face, it is bad manners to carry on a second conversation while on the telephone, unless it is obviously related to the call. If a third party can overhear our end of the conversation and the subject is sensitive, it is polite to make this clear.

'Actually I'm in a meeting just now'; or

'George is here with me at the moment'

may avoid later misunderstanding.

Covering the phone with a hand can usually be heard, and will cause suspicion. It is also a poor security device. Many modern telephones have a 'security' button which cuts off the microphone temporarily and is undetectable in operation.

Note it down

It is easy to forget the points covered during a conversation, and well-organised people keep paper and pen or pencil beside the phone. Some regular users keep a telephone journal in which they note the time, details of the other party and main points covered in all conversations.

Telephonists

The telephone may inspire people to talk more freely than when face to face, and with some the flow may become almost unstoppable. The subject may be relevant to the call, or mere gossip, but the consumption of time is the same. Stopping such people without causing offence can be tricky. Of course, it is inconceivable that we should suffer from the disease ourselves, or is it . . .?

Bad lines

These can cause much aggravation, apart from making conversation difficult. It is always worth suggesting a reconnection to see if a better line is available. If not, it may be better not to attempt to continue with an important discussion.

Making a call

Making a call is easier than receiving one. We have the initiative, and can set the scene and tone; but there are one or two common problems.

To wait or not to wait?

If an extension is busy, the telephonist will usually ask if we would 'like to hold'. To do so rarely helps, as it is time-consuming and expensive.

If the call is urgent, holding may be justified, but few things are more frustrating than hanging on during an apparently endless conversation which we cannot hear. We may think we are putting pressure on the person we need, but with most systems there will be nothing to tell him we are waiting. The only person under pressure is the telephonist, one of whose lines we are occupying; but he is usually powerless to help, and if we try to hurry him, friction may result.

Call back or leave a message?

If the person we want is not available, we can either leave a message or call back.

Telephone messages get lost or distorted, and are rarely given any degree of priority. Our circumstances may change before the call is returned and we may not need to speak after all. If we leave a message and then call back this can appear unduly pressing. If the recipient does not know us, it is usually better to keep control of the situation and say we will ring back.

If we do leave a message, it is best to leave our number, complete with code, even if we are sure the recipient already has it. He will be more likely to ring back if he does not have to search for the number.

Always reconnect
The caller should always ring back if disconnected, even if the conversation was nearly finished. This avoids any impression that the phone was slammed down out of pique.

Conclude neatly
It is natural for the caller to bring the call to a close. In doing so, he should leave no doubt as to what has been agreed, repeating any times or dates, and who is to take further action.

Telephone selling
The telephone is increasingly used for selling. Calls are made to possible buyers, either 'cold' or as a follow-up to a letter or circular. Some organisations specialise in such 'telesales' or 'telemarketing', carrying out campaigns for clients; in other cases the seller may use the technique direct.

Telephone selling is often based on a script which is designed to meet every likely situation or response by the recipient. It is an area which the interested reader should follow up through specialised publications or courses.

Receiving a call

Even receiving a telephone call allows scope for error and misunderstanding. Some potential problems are:

When to answer
It is best to let a phone ring two or three times before answering. Picking it up immediately will surprise the caller, and set the conversation off on the wrong foot.

On the other hand, a phone should not be left to ring for too long. This will upset the caller, occupy a line, and annoy everyone within earshot.

Identify ourselves
'Hullo', 'Yup', 'Can I help you?' are not good ways of answering the phone. The best answer depends on whether the phone (or extension) is exclusive, shared, or belongs to someone else. For one's own phone,

a friendly style is best, eg: 'Michael Green speaking'. 'Green' or 'Mr Green speaking' sound too curt and formal. However we answer, we must restrain our annoyance if the caller replies 'May I speak to Michael Green, please?'

If the phone is shared by several people, it is best to identify the office or function before giving one's name: 'Order Office, Michael Green speaking'.

If the phone is someone else's, and we just happen to be around, it is usual to say something like 'John Smith's telephone; may I help you?'

However we reply, we should speak clearly and not too fast.

Recognise people

Although conversations get off to a particularly good start if we indicate that we recognise the caller at once ('Hullo, Mr Brown! How nice to hear you') we shall cause offence if we get it wrong, so it is not worth running the risk if we have the slightest doubt.

Find out who is speaking

If the caller does not identify himself at once, we should ask who he is. The questions 'May I ask who is speaking?' and 'Who am I speaking to, please?' are always legitimate. If he also does not tell us the name of his organisation, we should continue with a question such as 'And your organisation, please?'

Note details

With paper and pen or pencil at the ready, we can note the name of the caller and any other details while we are talking. This will save having to ask him to repeat information, and we will be able to use the caller's name during and at the end of the conversation.

Transferring a call

Transferring a call from one extension to another is a potential source of difficulty.

The transfer sequence

A good sequence for transferring a call is:

1. Find out what the caller wants and who can help him best.
2. Explain that someone else is better able to help, say who, and tell the caller that you propose, with his agreement, to transfer him.
3. Speak to the other extension, explain what the caller wants and

who he is, and ensure the other extension is able and willing to help.

4. If all is well, complete the transfer.

Have numbers to hand

A list of telephone extensions or numbers, or an index or card box of information beside the phone, enables us to help callers quickly and impressively.

Multiple transfer

Few things are more annoying to a caller than to be transferred from extension to extension. If a call has been wrongly transferred, or the extension we thought was correct cannot help, it is best to tell the caller we will sort things out and ensure he is called back. The onus is then on us to check that the promise is kept.

Taking a message

Taking a telephone message is a deceptively simple act, and one with a high failure rate. Failures are always annoying, and can have serious consequences.

When to take messages

Taking a message is not always necessary. If we are able to do so, we should deal with the matter ourselves. For example:

'I'm afraid Mr Black isn't here today, but is there anything I can do to help?'

Occasionally, we will wish we had not offered, but we can always (and quite legitimately) fall back on:

'I'm sorry, but that's outside my field. Mr Black will be here in the morning and I will make sure he gets your message.'

More often, the enquiry will prove easy to handle, or can be passed to someone who *is* available.

The necessary information

Some organisations have telephone message forms, which act as checklists when taking messages. In the absence of these, we should note:

1. *Date and time* of the call. Time may be significant, so that receipt of the call can be related to other events. ('Did John ring before or after I called him?')

2. *Caller's name, organisation and, if offered, job title.*
3. *Caller's phone number, STD code and extension.*
4. *Message*, with as much detail as offered. We should try to understand as clearly as if we were handling the matter ourselves; nonsense messages help no one. (It does *not* give an impression of efficiency if the recipient has to begin his reply 'I got a garbled message that you called yesterday. What was it you wanted?' if the caller spent five minutes the previous day giving a perfectly lucid description.)
5. *An indication of the agreed follow-up.* This should make clear whether the caller will ring back or we are to ring him, and if so, when he will be available.
6. *Name of the person taking the message.*

The secretary's role

The secretarial telephone role traditionally includes spoon-feeding the boss ('I have Mr Brown for you') and protection ('Mr Green is in conference'). Neither does much to help effective communication. Defending a boss is delicate work requiring considerable sensitivity, and overprotective secretaries can be a source of friction with both staff and customers.

Outgoing calls
The staging of outgoing calls through a secretary is less common than it was, as most bosses now recognise that it is simpler and less pompous to get their own.

Incoming calls
Many phones now have the facility to divert unanswered calls to another extension after a short period, an arrangement which helps both caller and recipient.

Personal response
The most common form of secretarial response is:

> *'Mr Smith's office.'*

> *'John Smith's office, Mary Jones speaking'*

sounds friendlier and more personal, while:

> *'Mary Jones speaking'*

clearly indicates that Mary is an individual in her own right and not merely a hurdle on the road to Mr Smith.

Tone of voice

Tone of voice is critical for all telephone users, and secretaries can suffer from the occupational hazard of adopting a detached and unfriendly tone as part of their defensive role. At worst, this sounds as if it is intended to impress the importance of the boss on the caller and keep him in his place.

Such an approach not only generates friction and bad feeling, but also wastes time. Callers who feel they are being talked down to or fobbed off often fight back hard in an attempt to obtain a fair hearing.

Much better is the positive approach, in which both the tone of voice and the words used make it clear that we aim to do all we can to help the caller.

Asking questions

The secretary will need to ask questions, either as part of the defensive role or in order to be as helpful as possible. The way they are asked is important to the success of the conversation.

> *'May I ask what it is about?'*

may prove effective in pinning down someone we suspect to be a telephone salesperson, but it can also give offence to a hot prospect about to use our services for the first time, or an old college friend of the boss just arrived back from Australia.

> *'Is there any way I can help you?'*

can be a better first question.

If the caller is genuinely uncertain as to how to get what he needs, we will need to use tactful but thorough questioning, and to listen carefully to the answers. We must resist the temptation to transfer him to another extension just to get rid of him.

The boss's whereabouts

There are several traditional replies which amount, in practice, to the nineteenth-century maidservant's response to unwanted callers at the door: 'Her ladyship is not at home'. These include, in approximate order of unhelpfulness:

> *'He's taking a late lunch.'*

> *'He's with clients.'*

'*He's interviewing.*'

'*He's in a meeting.*'

'*He's in conference.*'

'*He's not in.*'

'*He's not available.*'

If the aim is to deter the caller, these may or may not succeed. If the aim is to help, they are inadequate; they give no guidance as to when he will be back, who might help now or what action is recommended.

A helpful response would be:

'*I'm afraid he's in a meeting at the moment. It should finish about 3 o'clock. May I ask him to ring you then, or is there anyone else who can help?*'

If in fact the boss is in, it is best to keep his and our options open by a non-committal

'*One moment, please*'

while we enquire whether the caller is to be put through or not.

Secretary to secretary

If the caller is another secretary whose boss wishes to speak to our boss, a power struggle may ensue to prevent the indignity of a boss speaking to a secretary. A simple approach is to say

'*Shall we go through together?*'

Special equipment

Telephones become more complex year by year. Many, but not all, of the complexities are designed to make them more user-friendly, but only to those users who take the trouble to learn about their capabilities. The telephone is in a state of continuous development, and we must not be left behind.

It is up to us to find out what our telephone can do, and what we must do to make full use of it. If other people work for us, we should help them to make proper use of their telephone facilities. User manuals should be freely available. It is important that everyone receives training when a new system is installed, and that newcomers are trained when they start.

Useful features

Many telephone systems have helpful features that are rarely used;

storage of numbers, or of the last number called; recall of an engaged extension when free, or of a 'no reply' extension on completion of its next call; diversion of all our calls, or when engaged, or after a set time without reply; 'group pick-up' facilities for several phones in the same department, and many others.

Mobile phones

The advent of mobile telephones has added further dimensions to using the phone. They can be of immense help, especially to sales staff and others who spend much time on the road. However, they also have drawbacks; they can disturb and distract drivers, meetings and other members of a theatre audience. They can find us when we do not wish to be found; taking a well-earned rest, perhaps, or concentrating on a difficult and urgent report. They are also expensive, not only to call from, but to call to, a fact which is not widely advertised. Before acquiring such equipment, we should consider all angles.

Telepaging devices, which receive and store messages in visual form, offer many of the advantages of mobile phones without the drawbacks.

Cordless phones, operating within a radius of about 50 yards, can be useful in situations where we do not spend the working day sitting at a desk.

Answering machines

These allow the user to relay a message to any caller as soon as he is connected, inviting him to leave a message which the machine will record.

The user can replay his messages at any time. Many machines and their messages can be accessed from a remote telephone, enabling the user to check his messages without returning to his office or home. They frequently have loudspeakers which can be set to amplify a call received while the user is present, and thus used to avoid responding to unwanted calls.

Some callers are put off when they hear an answering machine, although this is rarer as the machines become more common. Recent machines are also more reliable than earlier ones. One cause of reluctance is the feeling that messages may not be checked regularly or replied to quickly.

Answering machines have a great potential in telecommunication, and one which has not yet been fully exploited. They have particular value for one-person businesses. They can be useful for any telephone or extension where other arrangements for message-taking are difficult – even as a means of avoiding disturbance. They also seem likely to be used more and more frequently in the home.

The telephone – the top 20

The top 10 dos

1. Do 'put a smile in your voice'; sound warm and friendly.
2. Do ensure privacy when making a sensitive call.
3. Do note the caller's name and other details while speaking.
4. Do call back if, as caller, you are cut off.
5. Do identify yourself when making or answering a call.
6. Do check who is speaking if a caller does not say.
7. Do take great care when transferring a call.
8. Do keep extension numbers and other information to hand by the phone.
9. Do take and pass on messages promptly and accurately.
10. Do learn about and use the latest telephone technology.

The top 10 don'ts

1. Don't speak too loudly, too quietly or too fast.
2. Don't over-react to a caller's tone of voice.
3. Don't allow any phone to ring too long.
4. Don't carry on a second conversation.
5. Don't cover the phone with your hand.
6. Don't struggle with a bad line; call back.
7. Don't hold on for an extension.
8. Don't leave complicated or urgent messages if there is an alternative.
9. Don't allow unexplained silence during a call.
10. Don't chat on and on and on.

Chapter 11

Information Technology

Introduction

Information technology (IT) is probably the most rapidly developing area of technology today; however it is written, this chapter will be inevitably out of date in some way by the time you read it.

These developments have already had wide-ranging effects on both business and private life. All non-oral aspects of communication have become easier; letters, memos, reports, brochures of all kinds – even articles and books – can now be composed, produced, stored, accessed and distributed by machines with ever-growing efficiency and speed.

However, not all the effects have been beneficial. There is a danger of using technology simply to keep up with Jones plc next door, rather than to meet our own real needs. The IT industry has often been a world in which solutions have been in search of problems. Much money has been wasted and much harm done by the installation of equipment and systems that are unnecessary or inappropriate. Computers and IT have built a mystique with quite unnecessary jargon and user-unfriendly complexities, as if drivers were told they could not go on the road without understanding exactly how every piece of their car's machinery worked. The very speed of change creates major problems. Some people believe that there is now a danger of over-communication; the dream of the paperless office has, for many, become a nightmare of junk mail. The developments in IT are, however, so far-reaching that it is essential for us to keep up to date with them.

The uses of technology

Technology has a number of uses in handling information and thus helping communication. It can help in:

- collection
- storage

- processing
- transmission

and, to a very much lower extent, in

- using.

Collection

Before anything else can happen, information must be collected. Traditionally this has been a labour-intensive, person-based activity. Market surveys are carried out by interview; research is conducted in laboratories by technicians; books and journals are read by researchers; data is provided by individuals completing forms of all kinds.

Much of this collection activity continues, but increasingly technology is helping. Cameras and tape recorders collect information. Electronic sensors (for example of movement, temperature, sound) and devices capable of reading bar codes have become common. Electronic scanning of printed documents is increasingly used. Methods of voice-input, in which the spoken word is transformed automatically, are being developed. However, technology has so far made less impact in this area than in the others.

Storage

The classical means of storing information include: memory, paper records which are often held in filing systems, books and journals and card indexes. Technology has made substantial changes in this activity through micro-filming, gramophone records, electronic storage on tape, CD (compact disk), storage within computers (on 'hard disks') and on separate, so-called 'floppy' disks. Developments in this area continue at a fast rate. The CD-ROM (compact disk read-only memory) is still being developed for a range of applications, and even more powerful technologies are being examined.

Processing

Technology has given most help in the sorting and accessing of records. Before the general availability of computers and efficient software, cards with punched holes were developed that could be sorted manually by the use of needles. Mechanical sorting followed. In recent years cheap computers and the development of software has made the sorting of information held on electronic databases a simple and immensely powerful process.

Transmission

The human voice remains the prime means of transmitting information, but its leading position is eroded year by year. Postal services, telephone, radio and TV are now supplemented by telex, fax, tapes and disks, and the electronic transfer of information by many means. Cables (metal and now fibre-optic) and radio links (often using satellites) enable increasing volumes of information to be transmitted either generally or through networks. E-mail, a way of sending messages between computers, (electronic mail) is growing rapidly from being a locally based facility to a world-wide service.

It is in the field of transmission that technology is making the greatest contribution of all to communication.

Using

Using information must be the object of the whole exercise. Technology can play a part in this area in fully mechanical or automated systems, in which information is used to control what happens. Thus a train may be brought to a stand-still automatically by a danger signal or a valve closed when liquid in a tank reaches a predetermined level. However, using information is a characteristically human activity; life is based on continually making deductions and judgements on the information at our disposal. Attempts have been made to help or even replace this process with computer-based aids such as 'expert systems' and artificial intelligence (AI). These have helped in a few, specialised areas, but their practical applications have so far been limited.

The types of communication technology

Technology with particular relevance to business communication includes:

- computers
- audio
- video
- fax and telex
- photography
- public address systems.

Computers

As the name implies, computers were originally seen as calculating machines. Since their earliest practical applications, they have grown progressively smaller, more powerful and cheaper. The ways in which they store data have become more and more efficient. Word-processing, database spreadsheet, accounting and other software has been developed. All these, together with new telecommunications technology, have transformed computers into a highly efficient aid to communication. There are currently several main areas of development with which you should be familiar, namely:

Personal computers (PCs)

For many years, computers were large machines, requiring a special environment and expert use. The personal computer has for a number of years placed substantial and ever-growing computer power in the hands of individuals. They are now a key element in communication. With them, we can compose and print written documents of any size, from short memos to the longest book. 'Desk-top publishing' (DTP) software enables us to produce material to high standards of design and presentation suitable for printing. The 'hard disk' incorporated in the PC has the power to store large amounts of information. Individual 'floppy' disks provide indefinite capacity for storage, and can be filed and carried like cards. Communication with other PC users can be direct through modems, networks and E-mail, or by the physical transport of disks.

Laptops, or as they are often now called, 'notebook' computers can have the same power as desktop PCs, although they are readily portable. Together with portable printers and modems (which may both now be built in) they provide an immense enhancement of personal communicating power.

Even smaller, pocket-sized machines are available, and can be thought of as electronic calculators or organisers. These now have considerable power, and can often be linked to larger computers. However, many use special software, and all have, inevitably, small keyboards which limit their value for word-processing.

Networks

PCs and terminals for larger computers (sometimes called 'worksta-tions') are increasingly linked as part of a network. This provides the facility for immediate communication and the sharing of information (subject to any necessary safeguards) held at any point in the network. Networks may be confined to a single user or location, in which case they are known as LANs (Local Area Networks). LANs may, for example, link personnel within an office complex or a factory. A typical application is to connect sales staff with warehouses and accounts departments.

Larger, nationwide or even international networks called 'WANs' (wide area networks) can be dedicated to specific use by one or more organisation. Such networks are used extensively within the travel industry by travel agents and rail, air and bus operators. They are used by many financial institutions, especially banks and building societies, and are the basis of cashpoint machine operations. They are also used by the large supermarket chains so that the information from bar codes read at the checkout can be used not only to produce the customer's bill, but to update stock and financial records and initiate reordering when necessary.

LANs operate through cable connections between computers; it is now necessary to ensure that buildings have suitable cabling and ports built in. Larger networks depend on dedicated connections by landline or radio, possibly using satellites.

Ad hoc connection can also be achieved between any computers using modems – a device attached to a computer that, together with appropriate software, enables computers to use public telephone lines. They can be set up using the world-wide system known as Internet. With such technology it is already possible for computers to communicate virtually world-wide.

Such ease of communication has brought security problems. There have already been many cases of 'hackers' gaining unauthorised access to information. It is also possible for systems to be disrupted by outsiders. The introduction of the 'computer virus', capable of corrupting or destroying electronic records has caused serious difficulties.

E-mail

E-mail, or electronic mailboxes, uses computers with appropriate software to send messages to others. The messages can be to single or multiple recipients, and are stored on the receiving computer until called up. They can then be read on screen and, if wished, printed off. Mail can be protected by a password against unauthorised access.

Databases

A database is a set of records kept in a standard format. Non-electronic databases include card indices, telephone directories and files of application forms. The growth of computer technology has enabled such information to be held, processed and accessed electronically. Databases can be held within a computer, on its hard disk, on separate floppy disks and on CD-ROMs (see below). Depending on the capacity of the storage medium, the database may hold anything from a few hundred short records – such as a list of customers – to a library of technical data.

Databases may be for the use of the individual, for members of a permanent network, available to subscribers, or even accessible to all comers. Some organisations offer a 'gateway' service to their subscribers, with access on demand to a range of databases. Charges may be by subscription or raised automatically according to usage.

Databases already play a major part in some aspects of business. There are probably now over 5,000 worldwide, covering a broad range of subjects and a good proportion of published literature, either in the form of abstracts or full text. Some journals are now regularly published in electronic form. Directories are available listing databases currently available, but the situation is very fluid.

CD-ROM/multimedia

The CD-ROM is a compact disk used for storing information. 'ROM' stands for 'read only memory', meaning that the user cannot alter, add to or delete the information on the disk. The CD-ROM requires a special attachment or 'drive', which can be plugged into a PC or is, increasingly, supplied as standard equipment.

The capacity of the CD-ROM is very large. A single disk can hold about 250,000 A4 pages of text – enough for a full encyclopaedia. They are now used to carry specialist information such as technical manuals, legal and medical reference books, typographic and graphic design data. They are increasingly used to convey databases, which are regularly updated, to subscribers.

One of the most important developments in the use of CD-ROMs is in what has become known as 'multi-media' applications. These produce both on-screen images and sound. The images may use complex graphics, animation and incorporate video clips. The presentations may be interactive, in that the user can respond to questions or make choices which will determine what is shown. Such programmes have applications in training and education, and an increasing number of texts are available in CD format.

Benefits without problems

To reap the benefits of all types of computer-based IT while avoiding the problems mentioned at the start of this chapter, we must be prepared to challenge our thinking and that of others with questions.

Always ask yourself:

- What IT developments have occurred, or are being worked on, which might help my operation?
- Do developments suggest new things to do or new ways of doing things that would meet our overall objectives?

Before considering any specific new investment in IT:

- Am I certain the operations involved need doing at all?
- Could what we do be reduced or simplified?
- Could our present systems be eliminated or combined?
- Could information be shared between departments or systems?
- Are the operations done in the best place, at the best time, by the most suitable people?
- If we do invest in new IT, can we see any consequent problems such as lack of skills, additional costs, changeover difficulties, reduction in customer service and incompatibility with other systems?

Audio

The audio casette was first developed for business use, and only later adapted for music. It still has three uses in business communication:

- mobile note-taking
- dictation
- magazine tapes and 'talking books'.

Mobile note-taking
Pocket tape-recorders can be valuable in many situations. They can be used whenever a notebook would be clumsy or impossible to use: during site visits; in poor or non-existent lighting conditions; in public transport (for those who are not too self-conscious); while driving (with appropriate care); and at any time, such as in a crowded restaurant or in bed, when sudden inspiration may strike. They may also be used to record crucial meetings or conversations, although this may sometimes be seen as a form of eaves-dropping.

Dictation
Pocket tape-recorders are invaluable for those who need to dictate, especially at home, when travelling or otherwise away from the office. Purpose-designed transcription equipment is available for secretarial use in conjunction with tapes produced in this way.

The technique of audio dictating is described in Chapter 7, pages 130–31.

Magazine tapes and 'talking books'

A few magazines are issued in audio cassette form. An increasing number of books are published either solely on cassette or with a cassette as a supplement to the printed text. This medium is invaluable to the visually handicapped. It can add drama and interest and also provide illustrations in appropriate subjects, for example for books on bird calls or music. Tapes allow car drivers to put journey time to productive use.

Some tapes have also been produced for use during sleep as an aid to learning, or as an aid to relaxation.

Video

TV has found an increasing number of applications to business, in many cases replacing and extending the uses made of cine photography. These include:

- videotapes
- videotext
- closed circuit TV (CCTV).

Videotapes

The principal business application of pre-recorded videotapes is for training films. The format is more convenient than film for small and medium-sized groups, and can be used, with suitable projection equipment, for large audiences.

Some organisations with a number of sites use videotapes as a means of broadcasting information, recording and distributing presentations by senior staff for playback at remote locations. It is open to doubt whether such methods are as effective as face-to-face briefing by local management.

Videotext

The use of television channels and technology for the transmission of textual and graphic information is known as videotext. By this method, information of general interest, such as the latest cricket scores, weather forecast or road news, can be made widely available and updated regularly. There are several systems in the UK, including:

Teletext. This is the one-way broadcasting of textual material using spare television channel capacity. The user can receive this material on a TV set with the necessary additional equipment, and hold and read the pages at will. The BBC version is known as Ceefax, while ITV and Channel 4 transmit Teletext.

Viewdata also uses a television set, but the required pages of information are transmitted via a telephone line and modem. The British Telecom version of this is known as Prestel.

The applications for which this has proved appropriate and more efficient than written material are fewer than was at first thought.

Closed circuit TV (CCTV)

TV equipment is frequently used to communicate in a limited way, without broadcasting. Uses include:

- security observation
- process control and remote locations
- conferences and other meetings
- training.

Security observation. By using carefully placed cameras linked to a remote centre a small number of people can keep a range of locations under review. The system frequently includes a recorder which enables events to be re-examined, if necessary in slow motion or still frames, and possibly later used as evidence.

Such a system is helpful within shops, precincts and busy streets, the entrances and exteriors of buildings with a security risk, on railway platforms and crossings, and at road junctions. When first introduced, the cameras were regarded as a breach of privacy, but they are now more generally accepted, and the range and number of applications is continually growing.

Process control and remote locations. Cameras may be placed in locations which are difficult or even impossible for people to reach, due to temperature, physical danger, lack of space or remoteness. Combined with other technology such as telephoto lenses, fibre optics or radio links, their range can be extended to include such locations as missiles, satellites, space probes, the inside of pipework or even the living body.

With the help of such systems, tasks such as the control of complex production processes can be carried out by one person, and certain delicate surgical operations can be undertaken for the first time. The satellite and space applications have immensely important military functions, and when used for research have pushed back the frontiers of knowledge.

Conferences and other meetings. CCTV is frequently used to project moving images to a large audience. It can be used to communicate the proceedings in a packed meeting to those unable to get inside. It is now also used to project larger-than-life pictures of the current speaker, to ensure all have a close view of him, and to command greater attention.

Training. Videotapes are often used in place of film, especially for small groups. Video is easier to operate, does not require a blacked-out room, and the cassettes are easier to transport. It does not require development and can be replayed immediately.

Used in this way, CCTV is a valuable learning aid. The learner can watch a recording of his performance and view critical actions repeatedly – if necessary in slow motion or still frames. He can also store cassettes and observe his progress (or lack of it) at a later date.

When combined with a computer, CCTV can become interactive. If, for example, the learner answers a question in one way, a suitable sequence will be shown; if in another, a different sequence appropriate to his success or failure will follow. This technique is similar to but more direct and powerful than computer-aided learning.

Fax (Facsimile transmission)

Facsimile transmission can reproduce virtually any document of acceptable size at a distant location. Both sender and receiver must have a fax machine. Each machine can send and receive, and is connected to others by the telephone network, using numbers similar to or even the same as telephone numbers. The number of the receiver is dialled on a telephone and the document to be copied inserted. As the name implies, the system reproduces the appearance of the document, including all graphics, tables and layout. Correct receipt of documents can be confirmed immediately via the phone, and retransmission arranged if necessary.

Fax requires little training to operate; access to the equipment can be allowed to anyone within an organisation who needs it. It is flexible, relatively cheap and virtually automatic.

There are one or two weak points. The quality of reproduction is not always high, especially from poor originals. Transmitting longer documents is slow, and takes about 20 seconds a sheet. A machine can only send or receive at one time, and there may be queuing problems –

human or mechanical – while messages are processed. Fax is increasingly being used by marketers to send junk mail.

Fax combines the advantages of telex (see below) and ordinary mail, and competes in cost. It seems likely to continue growing as a means of documentary communication.

Telex

To communicate by telex, both sender and receiver need the special apparatus, and must be connected to the network. Like the telephone network, this is international and covers much of the developed world. Each terminal has a number similar to a telephone number. Messages are typed on a keyboard, and the receiving machine retypes them mechanically. Operating a telex requires some training.

Telex has the advantage of producing a clear, printed record at a distant location virtually instantaneously. This produces a record at each end which can be consulted in case of doubt or disagreement, and limits the danger of misunderstanding which can arise in a telephone conversation. However, the system does not produce facsimile messages, and cannot therefore reproduce drawings, graphs, tables, charts etc.

Photography

The camera has been a major aid to communication for over 100 years. There are four main applications:

- still photography
- cine photography
- microfilm
- microfiche.

Still photography
The increasing sophistication of photographic equipment has made still photography of much greater value in business communication. Three developments in particular have helped: colour photography, the instant camera and improvements in office copiers.

Colour photography. The ready availability of colour photography has made an immense change in the design and production of advertisements and brochures of all kinds. As a means of communication, its accuracy and the amount of information it can convey is much greater than black-and-white photography, and often superior to drawings or verbal descriptions. Its eye-appeal has virtually made it obligatory for all applications in which selling and persuasion are objectives.

Instant photography. The techniques of instant photography can be of great value when an immediate visual record is required, as, for example, in accidents, emergencies and all sorts of transient situations. They can be used to provide photographs of interview candidates to help interviewers' recall. The potential for business applications of such photography is probably not yet fully used.

Efficient office copiers. The value of still photography has also been increased by the ability of modern office copiers to reproduce them acceptably. We should always now consider using photographs not only in reports, but also in letters and memos.

Cine photography

Although cine photography has tended overwhelmingly to be used for entertainment, a few business applications have been developed. These include training films and high-speed photography of processes and events for analysis and record purposes.

The principal problems with cine photography have been the weight and size of the equipment, both cameras and projectors, and the need for expensive and time-consuming processing.

Cine photography has now been replaced in most business situations by video and closed circuit television.

Microfilm

For decades, the camera has been an aid to storing information by photographing documents on to reels of 35mm film – the size used by the majority of ordinary and cine cameras. After development, these can be accessed by means of a reading machine with a light, a lens and a ground glass screen.

Microfilm offers the advantage of vastly reduced storage space. It is particularly useful for archive copies of newspapers and other bulky documents such as invoices, receipts, application forms etc. However, these copies can only be accessed with a reader, and then only in the sequence in which they were photographed.

Microfiche

A variation of microfilm is microfiche. This is a flat sheet of film about five inches square on to which many pages of text –1000 or more – are photographed. The film can be stored flat, in files or between covers, along with paper, and it is possible to access the photographed pages in any order. Microfiche can thus be used for storing documents such as telephone directories, parts manuals and other reference books which would be virtually impossible to use on microfilm.

Much money and effort has been devoted to microfilm and microfiche. They have, however, considerable disadvantages. Preparation is costly and requires special equipment. Most people do not like using them, especially microfilm, where much time can be wasted searching for the required page. The need for a reading machine often leads to queues, which can be particularly frustrating for those wishing to make a quick, single reference.

While the investment already made means that microfilm and microfiche will be around for a long time, it has now been largely outmoded by electronic storage, and is unlikely to be a first choice for most applications.

Public address systems

Public address systems (often shortened to PA, or sometimes Tannoy, after a make of equipment) have an important but specialised role. PA is indispensable in communicating with crowds – especially outdoors, when on the move, or in disorganised groups as in supermarkets, railway stations, airports, sports grounds and outdoor rallies. It can also be useful for communicating with people spread over a number of locations – the shops and offices of an industrial plant, for example.

Situations in which PA is of the greatest value include:

- giving emergency instructions
- providing up-to-the-minute information on a changing situation
- drawing attention to other sources of information
- giving commentaries on sporting and other events
- playing background music
- advertising
- contacting individuals.

PA is usually at its best when supplementing other methods, such as arrival and departure boards and face-to-face communication.

Information technology – the top four

The top two dos
1. Do keep up to date on information technology of all kinds.
2. Do check how the latest technology affects your areas of interest.

The top two don'ts

1. Don't be bowled over by the latest gadgetry.
2. Don't allow salespeople to sell you hardware or systems you do not really need.

Chapter 12

Communicating Hardware

'Hardware' here refers to physical objects (other than books, papers and machines) which can be used to communicate. Some such objects may have other, more important uses, but it is their communicating role that interests us here. Communicating hardware includes:

- signs
- instrumentation
- notices and posters
- notice boards
- buildings and furniture
- clothing.

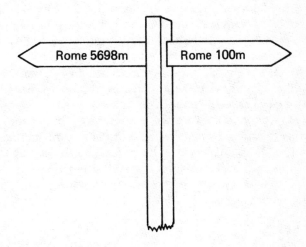

Signs

Devising road signs and signposts is the work of specialists, but the guidelines are the same for all signs:

- positioning
- size and style
- use of words or symbols
- sequence.

Other signs relating to movement – both outdoors or in, for vehicles or pedestrians – are a form of communication we are likely to use or devise in our working life. We need to ensure that visitors can get, for example, from the car park to reception, or find the loos, or we may be responsible for posting up signs communicating such messages as 'No smoking', 'Private, staff only', 'Mind your head' and 'Please keep off the grass'. We may even be involved in the signposting of a complex area such as a supermarket, hospital or factory. The skill with which we carry out such tasks has a big effect on our relationships with customers, other visitors and staff.

The *company logo* probably deserves a mention here. As a sign it appears on premises. Adapted, it is used on stationery, publicity material and advertisements, uniforms and transport, promoting the corporate image to the public.

Positioning

Positioning must not only attract attention at the right time, but also, unlike many statutory parking restriction signs, make for easy reading. A change of a few inches can make all the difference. (One day, perhaps, the authorities involved will realise that most drivers sit with their heads about four feet above the road surface, not six.)

The effects of both natural and artificial light in differing conditions and at different times of day are also important; we may need to consider the provision of lighting.

Clutter is often caused by too many signs, notices and posters clamouring for attention and making effective communication by any of them less likely. This may be as a result of different individuals or bodies competing for limited attention or territory, but is more often lack of co-ordination or simply lack of common sense. There is no point in adding yet another sign if it will not be read.

Size and style

The size and style must be suitable for attracting attention, but not such as to dominate the environment. The use of a standard style for a set of signs can help.

Clear words or symbols

A mixture of clear upper and lower case lettering, as used in motorway

Non-verbal signs

and railway signs, is more legible than all capitals.

Many signs are now produced in non-verbal format (eg the signs used for women's and men's toilets). When well designed in suitable applications, symbols speed understanding, help the partially sighted and illiterate, and overcome language barriers. Symbols can also be used in addition to a verbal message.

The pictograms used on crates, cartons and packing cases are in the same class. Messages such as 'keep dry', 'this way up', 'delicate', or 'use no hooks' are conveyed immediately to all concerned, whatever verbal language they speak.

Sequence

When erecting direction signs we must, by definition, be familiar with the route and the local geography, and may therefore have difficulty in understanding the problems of a stranger. There is little point, for example, in leading people safely, as so many signs do, to a junction within a short distance of the destination and then abandoning them. To locals, the end of the route is easy – but signs are not erected for locals.

Instrumentation

The use of instruments to communicate has assumed ever greater importance as technology of all kinds has expanded. Until the last century, the only familiar example was the use of clock dials to tell the time. Today, most of us are at home reading the messages conveyed by car instrumentation, the faces of radios and other electronic machinery. Instrumentation is, of course, a vital component of industrial communication.

Analogue and digital instruments

There has been an opposite change in the language of instrumentation to that of signs; it has tended to move from 'analogue' to 'digital'.

Analogue instruments convey a message by the changing relation-

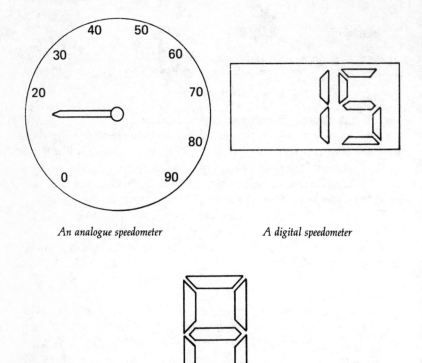

An analogue speedometer   *A digital speedometer*

The arrangement for a numeric digital display

ship or visible shape of their components; the best-known example is the clock face with its circular dial and hands of different lengths. Many instruments, such as speedometers and aircraft altimeters, were for many years based on the same principle.

The development of electronics has produced a growing number of digital instruments which convey their message by a direct readout of figures. Arabic numerals are now a virtually worldwide language. The brilliantly simple discovery that they could all be represented by combinations of seven suitably arranged bars made electronically controlled numeric displays simple to design and use. Electronics has also made far more accurate measurement of many variables possible. Digital watches and clocks are now common, and many other instruments, particularly in industrial applications, are now designed in this way.

Notices and posters

A range of statutory notices, certificates, licences and similar documents must by law be displayed in specified situations.

These include items such as summaries of the Offices, Shops and Railway Premises Act, certificates of Employer's Liability Insurance, partnership and company notices. There are, in fact, few business premises in which a number of such notices should not be on display.

Such notices communicate little to most people, except 'you have been warned'. As a means of passing information, they must rate as next to useless, being couched in language that most readers have neither the training nor the inclination to understand. Often, their only message is for the various officials who have a right of entry and inspection, to indicate that their instructions have been carried out.

Office notice boards

Most organisations rely on notice boards for a variety of purposes. The armed forces use them as a principal channel of communication, through which both standing and daily orders are passed. In Civvy Street, it is unwise to assume that more than a small proportion of those affected will read the notice board.

Notice boards are effective in communicating simple, immediate messages. They are ideal, for example, for conveying a welcome to important visitors when they step into reception, or warning railway passengers about tomorrow's one-day strike.

The effectiveness of notice boards depends on how they are kept. They respond well to tender loving care, and rapidly become useless if left to their own devices. They are at their best when notices are carefully selected and positioned, and ruthlessly removed when their job is done.

Memos are often displayed on notice boards to ensure general communication of their message. If written with this in mind, they may perform the extra function well, but to be fully effective, notices require thought in their own right.

The requirements for an effective notice are: a clear heading; a few brief and clearly expressed points; an indication of where to obtain additional information, and the date of posting.

Clear heading

The purpose of the heading is to catch the eye of potential readers and to focus their thoughts on what follows. It must, therefore, use simple language and be brief, accurate, clear and large enough to be read easily from a distance. A mixture of upper and lower case lettering (as used for the headings on this page) is easier to read than unmixed capital letters.

Few brief and clearly expressed points

Complex and lengthy notices may meet the requirements of the law but they will neither be read nor understood by most people. To communicate, the message of a notice must be expressed in a few (preferably no more than five) brief 'bullet' points. The sequence of the points must be logical, and each must use simple language.

Where to obtain additional information

Notices should always show clearly who is responsible for the message they give and who, therefore, can answer questions or deal with any response. The internal telephone number and office location will usually be necessary.

The date of posting

The date draws readers' attention to the recency or otherwise of a notice, enables them to relate it to other communications they may have had on the same subject, and guides whoever is responsible for the notice board as to when it should be removed. Like yesterday's newspaper, a board covered with old notices is seldom read.

An example:

Christmas Arrangements

- *This office will be closed from 1500 on 22 December until 0800 on 2 January.*

- *The telephone switchboard will not be manned during this period, but the answering equipment will be in operation.*

- *Anyone requiring access during this period* must *contact me before 1000 on 21 December.*

Julia Pink   *20 November 1990*
Office Services Manager
Room 123
Ext 254

Posters inform or advertise. They need to be legible, whether the passer-by is whizzing past in a train or walking along the pavement.

This reduces the use of words, and places greater emphasis on design, layout and illustration. The first objective is to gain attention.

Buildings and furniture

In the past, the outsides of buildings were often designed to communicate messages such as civic pride, stability, success, wealth or functional efficiency. Such communication has become rarer in recent years – it is difficult to project an organisational personality through the architecture of the industrial estate and the business park. The strongest message is now usually conveyed by the public parts of the interior. It is to the entrance foyers, reception desks, corridors and lifts of modern business architecture that we must look for any messages about the organisation.

Professor Northcote Parkinson, in his immortal *Parkinson's Law*, suggests that buildings may be a useful guide as to which companies are likely to be the soundest investment. He compares a company whose headquarters is housed in a brand-new and palatial building, complete with every convenience, with one housed in Nissen huts in the back garden of a Victorian terraced house. Perhaps surprisingly, he suggests that the second would be a wiser investment. The first, he argues, has plateaued out after a period of growth, and can only go downhill; it is suffering from 'ingelilitis'. The second, on the other hand, is in the early stages of a period of dynamic growth, and represents a wise choice for the investor.

The message that buildings communicate is also affected by the remainder of a site, including gardens, yards and car parks. If these are unplanned or neglected, they can do much to harm an organisation's image in the eyes of staff, customers and the whole company.

Furniture
Furniture communicates both in its own right and by virtue of how it is arranged. In its own right, it can indicate wealth or lack of it, working priorities, artistic taste, social background, real or would-be status, personal history and a range of other information.

In all but the most rigid organisations, individuals can move furniture around to meet situations as they see them, and the way we choose to do so is related to the way we work. The way furniture is arranged can have a big effect on the atmosphere and efficiency of meetings (page 96) and interviews (pages 117 and 118).

With office furniture, the most important factor is the placing of the desk. The position relative to the door, the window and the walls suggests a good deal about the occupant. A desk placed squarely near the middle of an office and with the window directly behind it may suggest that the occupant wishes to maintain a formal relationship with others; possibly that they are anxious to impress others with their status.

On the other hand, a desk placed against the wall suggests an occupant who aims to establish open relationships with fellow workers and who feels no need of a defensive barrier.

Clothing

Swift said that 'the tailor makes the man'. Certainly, most of what we see of others (holiday beaches excepted) is clothing.

The clothes we wear communicate:

- authority and rank (peaked hats, gold braid)
- occupation (chef's hat, butcher's apron)
- attitude of mind (kiss-me-quick and paper hats)
- religious beliefs (monk's habit, bishop's gaiters)
- current role (bridal dress, Ascot hat)
- political and other affiliation (club blazers and ties, black shirts)
- activity (cricket flannels, tracksuit).

Clothing also communicates on a more personal level; it is possible to deduce from it taste, social background, attitudes and group affiliation. Sherlock Holmes could, according to Conan Doyle, tell most of a man's life history from his clothes.

Much clothing is chosen, especially in a working context, from pure convention. If, as a male executive, we wear a sober blue suit, shirt and tie we tell the world nothing except that we accept the uniform for the job. The same is true of the youngster in the disco wearing jeans and a bright, open-necked shirt.

The individual wearing a suit at the disco or jeans in the office would convey a stronger message. However, even such breaks with convention may have trivial reasons; our only suit may be at the cleaners, or we may have just stepped off a plane from Hong Kong. The fact is that, particularly for males, business clothing is a uniform over which we exercise little control.

Clothing for customer contact

One aspect of clothing is of considerable practical importance in a business context: the effect of the clothing worn by personnel in direct contact with customers. Some organisations leave choice to individual taste, some give general guidance, some offer clothing for those who want it, and some issue and expect employees to wear uniform.

The choice of clothing that communicates effectively with the customer, while being acceptable to the wearers, is a matter for the most careful thought. It can express corporate image and identity, and will suggest how the organisation views its customers.

Whatever choices are made, the views of those who must wear the clothing are important. If it helps them both to look and feel good they will communicate these feelings to the customer.

Needless to say, the fit, cleaning and maintenance of such clothing needs as much attention as the original choice.

Uniform

Wearing a uniform is essential in certain sectors such as the police and armed forces. It is also of practical assistance to others such as commissionaires, airline cabin staff, waiters and car park attendants. However, its connotations of authority and uniformity are repugnant both to some employees and some customers, and its use needs care.

Communicating hardware – the top 20

The top 10 dos

1. Do display sufficient signs to help visitors.
2. Do choose the style and wording of signs for maximum clarity and to create a house style.
3. Do consider the effects of natural and artificial lighting of signs.
4. Do use symbols in preference to or in addition to words.
5. Do ensure that direction signs are provided at all points of doubt.
6. Do keep notice boards neat and up to date.
7. Do consider the effects of furniture and its arrangement in foyers, meeting and interview rooms, and offices.
8. Do consider the image created by car parks, loading bays, yards, gardens and other external areas of a site.
9. Do choose clothing for customer-contact staff with great care.
10. Do use the company logo to good promotional effect.

The top 10 don'ts

1. Don't use complex or lengthy wording on signs and notices.
2. Don't leave gaps in sequences of direction signs.
3. Don't produce clutter by displaying too many notices close together.

4. Don't assume notice boards will be read; provide back-up communication for important matters.
5. Don't leave outdated notices on display.
6. Don't allow furniture or its arrangement to be a barrier to effective communication.
7. Don't choose intimidating uniforms for customer-contact staff.
8. Don't neglect the cleaning and care of uniforms and other clothing of customer-contact staff.
9. Don't forget the value of the company logo, pictures and other artefacts in creating a positive organisational image.
10. Don't neglect the cleaning and upkeep of all public areas of premises and site.

Further Reading

Chapter 1. The Elements of Communication
The Handbook of Communication Skills, Bernice Hurst, Kogan Page, 1991
Guide to Managerial Communication, Mary Munter, Prentice Hall, 1992

Chapter 2. Face to Face
Business Etiquette: your complete guide to correct behaviour in business, David Robinson, Kogan Page, 1994
Agreed!: how to make your management communication persuasive, Patrick Forsyth, Kogan Page, 1993
Tough Talking: how to handle awkward situations, David Martin, Pitman, 1993
Interpersonal Skills: goal-directed behaviour at work, John Haynes, HarperCollins Academic, 1991

Chapter 3. Interviews
Great Answers to Tough Interview Questions, 3rd edn, Martin John Yate, Kogan Page, 1992
Readymade Interview Questions, Malcolm Peel, Kogan Page, 1989
Professional Interviewing, Rob Miller, Valerie Crute and Owen Hargie, Routledge, 1992
Successful Interviewing in a Week, Mo Shapiro, Headway, 1993
Succeed at Your Job Interview, George Heaviside, BBC Books, 1993
Winning at Your Interview, Michael Stevens, Kogan Page, 1990

Chapter 4. Oral Presentation
Successful Presentation in a Week, Malcolm Peel, Headway, 1992
Effective Presentation, Anthony Jay, Pitman, 1993
Public Speaking in Business, Stuart Turner, McGraw Hill, 1991
The Business Guide to Effective Speaking, Jacqueline Dunckel and Elizabeth Parnham, Kogan Page, 1985

Chapter 5. Meetings

Effective Meeting Skills, Marion E Haynes, Kogan Page, 1988
How to Make Meetings Work, Malcolm Peel, Kogan Page, 1988
How to Organise Effective Conferences and Meetings, 4th edn, David Seekings, Kogan Page, 1989
How to Take Minutes of Meetings, Jennie Hawthorne, Kogan Page, 1993
Let's Have a Meeting: a comprehensive guide to making meetings work, Leslie Rae, McGraw Hill, 1994

Chapter 6. The Media Face to Face

Media Interview Technique: handling the media and getting your point across on TV, radio and within your organisation, Peter Tidman, McGraw Hill 1992
Surviving the Media Jungle: a practical guide to good media relations, Dina Ross, Mercury Books, 1990

Chapter 7. Letters, Memos and Other Office Communications

The Business Guide to Effective Writing, John Fletcher and David F Gowing, Kogan Page, 1989
Successful Business Writing in a Week, Gordon Wainwright, Headway, 1993
Perfect Business Writing: all you need to know to get it right first time, Peter Bartram, Century Business, 1993
Readymade Business Letters that Get Results, 2nd edn, Jim Douglas, Kogan Page, 1994

Chapter 8. Reports and Brochures

The Business Guide to Effective Writing, John Fletcher and David F Gowing, Kogan Page, 1989
Report Writing, Joan van Emdem, Jennifer Easteal, McGraw Hill, 1993
Report Writing in Business, Trevor J Bentley, Kogan Page, 1988
The Secrets of Successful Business Report Writing, Clive Goodworth, Butterworth Heinemann, 1991

Chapter 9. News Releases and Advertising

How to Write Sales Copy that Really Sells, Mark Hempshell, Thorsons, 1992
The New How to Advertise, Kenneth Roman and Jane Mass, Kogan Page, 1992
Writing to Sell: the complete guide to copywriting for business, Kit Sadgrove, Robert Hale, 1991

Chapter 10. The Telephone

Customer Service: how to achieve total customer satisfaction, Malcolm Peel, Kogan Page, 1993

The Power of the Phone: tested techniques to cut costs, save time and boost sales, Pat Cochrane, Pitman, 1993

Successful Telephone Techniques, Judith Taylor, 1994

Tame that Phone: controlling the tyranny of the telephone, Polly Bird, Pitman, 1994

Chapter 11. Information Technology

Information Technology in Business: an introductory textbook, Roger Brady, Stanley Thornes, 1991

The Organized Executive: 101 ways to manage time, paper and people, 2nd edn, Stephanie Winston, Kogan Page, 1994

Index